BARBECUE & SMOKE COOKERY

BY MAGGIE WALDRON

DRAWINGS BY ERNI YOUNG

101 PRODUCTIONS, SAN FRANCISCO

TO KATIE AND GENE

Portions of this book were previously published
by 101 Productions under the title *Fire & Smoke*

Copyright © 1978, 1983 Maggie Waldron
Drawings copyright © 1978, 1983 Erni Young

Published by 101 Productions
834 Mission Street
San Francisco, California 94103

Library of Congress Cataloging in Publication Data

Waldron, Maggie, 1927-
    Barbecue and smoke cookery.

    New ed. of: Fire & smoke.
    Includes index.
    1. Barbecue cookery. 2. Outdoor cookery.
    3. Cookery, International. I. Title.
TX840.B3W34 1983   641.7'6   82-24683
ISBN 0-89286-211-4

CONTENTS

 # ABOUT FIRE & SMOKE

Here's to Captain Kidd and that other rogue of a pirate, Long John Silver—who was nicknamed "Barbecue"—for the gastronomic revelry that is part and parcel of the world of charcoal cooking. Those greedy, gusty buccaneers lived among the Arawak Indians, *boucaning* (and that's the origin of "buccaneer") the game and fish of the islands over the *barbacoa,* a frame of thin green sticks over which the game was grilled on an open fire. When the French corsairs dubbed this culinary adventure *de barbe et queue,* which translates "from beard to tail," the most primitive form of feasting was named.

ON CHARCOAL FIRES

Charcoal briquettes from a hardwood or fruit-pit base are for me the best and most efficient fuel. Keep them dry. Build them pyramid fashion, kindle with an odorless fire starter, and let them burn for half an hour or more until they glow with a white ash. Push the coals into what I call a *smoke ring,* an oval roughly the shape of whatever you are cooking. This method keeps the coals from flaring up and allows you to keep a drip pan under the meat to collect the precious juices—and you can set planks of thick bread in the drip pan for *lèchfrite,* or "lick fry" as they say in Switzerland, to catch the drippings and serve as beds for game birds or sliced meat.

Always avoid making the fire too big. The size of the food to be cooked should determine the dimensions of the fire. A portable grill might only take fifteen or twenty briquettes, while a larger unit will take forty-five. By using the smoke ring, you can bring your fire up very close to whatever you are cooking without inducing flame, and this is the best way to control heat.

The best spit-roasting temperatures range from 225° to 350°F, with beef generally taking a higher temperature, lamb, pork, and poultry a medium one, and fish one in the low range. Grilling temperature is always higher than that for spit roasting and should be around 350° to 400°F at grill level. If you have no grill thermometer, hold your palm down near the grill and count seconds. If you can count to three, the fire is just about right. If it's hotter than that, wait a bit or space out the coals. If you can hold your hand in place for eight seconds, push the coals together, knock off some of the ash, or add more coals to boost the fire power. (When you add coals during cooking, always add them at the edge of the fire, away from the food.) Again, as with spit roasting, most cuts of beef take the hottest fire, while other meats and seafood do best on a less intense one. A general rule of thumb is to place the grill about six inches from the coals for most cooking situations. Adjust the distance according to whether you want to cook foods more quickly or slowly.

A pit thermometer, with which some grills are now equipped, is invaluable, and so is a meat thermometer, especially the one that reads from zero to 220°F like my Taylor, which takes an instant reading. Cooking times given in this book are meant to be a guide only, as the degree of heat of the fire, the thickness of the cut of meat, the amount of draft, and the like are all critical factors. As you do more charcoal cookery, judging cooking times will become easier.

SPIT ROASTING

The most important thing to remember when spit roasting is that the meat must be securely balanced on the spit. Failing this, the meat will cook unevenly. Insert the meat on the spit and then test the balance by giving the spit a few turns before beginning the cooking. If the action is smooth, without any jerking motion or flapping of the meat, the food will cook evenly. Irregularly shaped roasting meats may require the use of a specially

designed weight to aid in the balancing. The roasting meat should be positioned so that the top moves away from the cook, and the drip pan should be placed in the front of the pit for easy access by the cook. It is generally best to use a meat thermometer for testing for doneness.

SMOKE COOKING AND THE CHINESE SMOKE COOKER

Smoke cooking and smoking are two different processes, although the ancient Chinese "beehive" method where the meat hangs in a chimney well away from the coals combines the two methods, the hot smoke imparting the flavor. Cold smoking is more of a curing process, which takes days and uses little heat. There are several smoke oven units currently on the market. The greatest advantage to smoke cooking is, of course, the definite smoky flavor the food takes on. Additional advantages are the ability to maintain an even temperature because it is a covered cooking system, and the convenience of "baking" the rest of your meal—a covered casserole, baked potatoes, etc.—right alongside your "barbecued" course. For more information on smoke cooking, see the chapter beginning on page 160. The beginning section, "Cooking with Smoke," discusses smoke cooking versus smoke roasting or grilling, and cold smoking.

AROMATIC SMOKES

Hickory chips and fruit woods (which have first been soaked in water) can be put on the fire early in the cooking or later (see "Cooking with Smoke" on page 160, about wood). As you look through this book, you'll find suggestions for aromatics used in the various countries—tea and orange peel in China, herbs and grapevines in France, a handful of garlic cloves and branches of bay leaf in Italy. Generally, whatever is available and smells good to you with whatever you're cooking can be tossed on the hot coals.

ON SEASONING

The salt-broiling technique of Japan (page 135) breaks down the fat under the skin of fish and chicken and keeps the flesh moist during the cooking. Otherwise, it's better to wait until the meat is almost done before salting, as it causes the juices to run. A coarse salt grinder and pepper grinder are absolute musts. The charcoal flavor is seasoning in itself, but the aromatic herbs and spices are excellent when used with discretion. Game birds may have been feeding on strong wild herbs such as sage, which will affect the flavor. The stronger herbs, or "potherbs," are marjoram, basil, mint, sage, rosemary, thyme, tarragon, dill, oregano, and bay. The milder herbs are savory, chervil, chives, and parsley.

ON EQUIPMENT

Historically, charcoal cooking has not only been possible but probable under the most primitive of conditions. The very best food I've had has been cooked over the simplest grills and contraptions. I'm more concerned with a few useful tools.

A good larding needle, twelve to fifteen inches long Essential for adding fat to fowl and game, which tend to have much less fat than their domestic counterparts, and for some cuts of veal and lamb.

Basting brushes and a suction baster The brushes are good for thicker bastes and the suction baster for marinades.

A few good tongs and chopsticks Far better than forks, which pierce the flesh of meat and vegetables, and they are available in several sizes and weights to fit the particular job.

A flexible filleting knife High quality and always sharp, this is essential for filleting fish.

Hinged grills and broiling baskets I have found one for small fish, one for a big fish and a couple for whatever seems right.

A "spitless" spit There's nothing like a rotisserie for cooking large cuts of meat and whole birds, and nothing like this linked metal basket that secures the meat on a spit without the need for points, prongs, or forks. You can also do whole fish by the rotisserie method in this basket, available through your barbecue equipment supplier.

Skewers Again, I like an assortment: heavy ones with wooden handles, long ones that will take a whole meal of a *shish kebab,* short ones that grill the hors d'oeuvre, bamboo sticks for certain foods (always soak them in water so they won't burn), two-tined skewers or forks with long wooden handles for toasting marshmallows and such.

A squirt bottle The kind you sprinkle your clothes with, to keep filled with water by the side of the fire to douse any flare-ups.

Asbestos gloves, towels and heavy-duty pot holders, a nest of trays, heavy-duty foil, pancake turners, fowl shears, garlic press, and good sharp knives.

BARBECUE TIMING CHART
Charcoal and Gas Kettles

STEAKS AND KEBABS
mps = minutes per side
1 inch thick: rare=3-4 mps, med=4-5 mps, well=5-6 mps
1-1/2 inches thick: rare=5-6 mps, med=7-8 mps,
  well=9-11 mps
2 inches thick: rare=7-8 mps, med=9-10 mps,
  well=10-12 mps
1-1/2-inch cubes: med=10-15 mps

HAMBURGERS
mps = minutes per side
3/4 inch thick: rare=3 mps, med=4 mps, well=5 mps
1 inch thick: rare=4-5 mps, med=5-6 mps, well=6-7 mps

ROASTS
Important: Plan to let all roasts stand 20 minutes before carving. Roasts continue to cook during this period and the internal temperature will rise about 10°F. (Example: For rare beef remove from heat at 130°F.)

BEEF ROASTS
Temperature when cooked: rare=140°F, med=160°F,
  well=170°F
Cooling time given in minutes per pound, unless otherwise noted
Rib roast, 6-8 lb.: rare=16-18 mpp, med=18-20 mpp,
  well=20-22 mpp
Rib eye, 4-6 lb.: rare=16-18 mpp, med=18-20 mpp,
  well=20-22 mpp
Tenderloin, whole, 4-6 lb.: 40-60 min. total time
Rump, rolled, 4-6 lb.: 18-22 mpp

LAMB ROASTS
Temperature when cooked: rare=140°F, med=160°F,
  well=170°F
Cooking time given in minutes per pound
Leg, 5-9 lb.: rare=18-22 mpp, med=22-28 mpp,
  well=28-33 mpp
Leg, boneless, 4-7 lb.: rare =22-28 mpp, med=28-33 mpp,
  well=33-38 mpp
Shoulder, square cut, 4-6 lb.: med=22-28 mpp,
  well=28-33 mpp
Shoulder, boneless: rare=28-33 mpp, med=33-38 mpp,
  well=38-43 mpp
Rib, 2-3 lb.: rare=25-30 mpp, med=30-35 mpp,
  well=35-40 mpp

PORK ROASTS
Temperature when cooked=170°F
Cooking time given in minutes per pound
Loin, center, 3-5 lb.: 25-30 mpp
Loin, half, 5-7 lb.: 30-35 mpp
Leg (fresh ham) bone in, 12-16 lb.: 18-24 mpp
Leg (fresh ham), boneless, 5-8 lb.: 18-24 mpp
Half, 5-8 lb.: 25-30 mpp
Tenderloin, 1/2-1 lb.: 45-60 min. total time

BAKED HAM
Temperature when cooked=140°F for fully cooked,
  160°F for uncooked
Cooking time given in minutes per pound
Ham, fully cooked: 8-10 mpp
Ham, uncooked, whole, 10-14 lb.: 12-18 mpp
Ham, uncooked, half, 5-7 lb.: 12-18 mpp

CHOPS, RIBS, AND VARIETY MEATS
Important: Take care that the heat is not too hot. Chops, ribs, and variety meats dry out easily.

CHOPS AND RIBS
1 inch thick: 12-15 min. each side
2 inches thick: 20-25 min. each side
Back ribs: 1-1/2 - 2-1/2 hr. total time
Spareribs: 45-60 min. total time
Country-style ribs: 1-1/4 - 1-3/4 hr. total time

VARIETY MEATS
Sweetbreads, any weight: 10-15 min. total time
Kidneys, any weight: 10-15 min. total time
Lamb/veal heart, whole: 10-15 min. total time
Lamb tongues, 5 oz. each: 15-20 min. total time
Liver steaks, 1/2 inch thick: 2-4 min. total time
Whole liver, 2 inches thick: 20-30 min. total time

FISH
Important: Cook fish 10 minutes per inch (thickness measured at thickest point) or when flesh is opaque when flaked with a fork.
Lobster: 10-20 min. total time
Mussels: 3-5 min. total time
Oysters: 3-5 min. total time
Scallops: 5-10 min. total time
Shrimp: 5-10 min. total time

POULTRY
Important: Plan to let poultry rest 20 minutes before carving. Internal temperature will rise by about 10°F.
Temperature when cooked: 185°F
Cooking time given in minutes per pound
Capon, 5-8 lb.: 15-20 mpp
Chicken, 2-1/2 - 3-1/2 lb.: 18-20 mpp
Duck, 4-6 lb.: 12-15 mpp
Goose, 8-12 lb.: 30-35 mpp
Rock Cornish hens, 3/4 - 1-1/2 lb.: 45-60 min. total time
Turkey, 8-16 lb.: 15-20 mpp
Turkey, 16-25 lb.: 12-15 mpp

VEGETABLES
Belgian endive, split heads: 15-20 min.
Corn on the cob (in moistened husks): 15-20 min.
Eggplant, peeled and cut into 1-inch cubes or slices:
  10-15 min.
Garlic, parboiled, whole buds: 10-15 min.
Mushrooms, large: 8-12 min.
Potatoes, whole, baked in coals: 45-60 min.
Potatoes, parboiled thick slices: 10-15 min.

NORTH AMERICA

For many years, the Eskimos and Indians of the Arctic regions of the world have met to compete in athletic games unique to their own villages. The first Eskimo Olympics was held in Fairbanks in 1961, and since then the six major Eskimo and Indian tribes in Alaska, the Eskimos, Aleuts, Tsimpshians, Tlingits, Haidas, and Athabascans, have met to compete in games such as the high kick, knuckle hop, ear pull, blanket toss, seal hook throw, seal skinning. There is also at these affairs much dancing and, of course, eating. I lived in Fairbanks for a cold spell and was one of the privileged few outsiders to compete in the blubber-eating or muktuk contest, which took place with some 200 contestants flat on a cold gym floor with hands behind back. I have never forgotten that ordeal but I remember with relish the incredible fish from the icy waters, still crisp on the inside after being cooked over the coals.

ALASKAN SPLIT-LOG GRILL

Fish, steak, or any meat can be cooked this way. Thick pieces of meat will have to be turned over to finish cooking. Split a piece of firewood that is at least 6 inches in diameter and soak the wood in water. Place the meat on the flat side of one half of the split piece. Outline the meat on wood at intervals with nails. Lace with string from nail to nail across the meat to hold it in place. Sharpened wooden pegs can also be nailed into the meat to hold it in place. Place the meat toward the fire.

ESKIMO FISH-ON-A-STICK WITH WILD BLUEBERRIES

Clean your fish, leaving its head on. Sharpen both ends of a sweet-bark stick about the circumference of your finger and 6 inches longer than the fish. Thrust one end of the stick through the fish's mouth, up inside near the backbone, and into the flesh of the tail. Rub the fish with corn or other vegetable oil. Wrap foil around the exposed end of the stick to prevent it from burning. Push the free end of the stick into the ground near the fire until fish's head nearly touches the ground. Push the coals toward the stick and cook fish until it flakes. Serve with crushed blueberries with a little sugar and lemon juice added to taste.

Of all the exceptional seafood of Chesapeake Bay —rockfish, bluefish, herring, and hardheads—shad is the tastiest of all. A popular, long-cooking method is to wrap the buck shad in brown paper or foil, and cook slowly in a smoke oven for five or six hours. It has fatter, firmer flesh than the roe shad. And the old-timers like to grill the roe, too.

SHAD AND SHAD ROE

4 small shad fillets
2 pairs shad roe
1 lemon
1/4 pound butter
Salt and freshly ground pepper
Finely chopped parsley

Place each of the fillets on a foil rectangle. Split the roe and set one on each of the fillets. Squeeze lemon juice over all. Dab with butter. Sprinkle with salt and pepper and parsley. Bring the foil up over the roe to form a tight package and fold up the ends. Cook on the grill 18 minutes, or until fish flakes easily. Serve in the foil packages so none of the juices are lost.
Makes 4 servings

Our only true, native cuisine is that of our fish and shellfish. It has resisted the passage of time and the influence of Europe and the Orient. It is plain and straightforward and honest-to-God *fresh*. The ancient Indian clambake is probably the best example of an all-American ritual that combines the best of all worlds.

AN ALL-AMERICAN CLAMBAKE

You must start early in the morning to dig the clams and gather the groceries for this big feed. Split up the chores: Firewood and stones are stacked in a neat rectangular pile. The clams are washed and soaked in fresh water to spit out the sand. The fresh fish is cleaned, salted, and wrapped in paper bags. Onions are peeled, corn is shucked at the last minute, lobsters and crabs are rinsed in clear sea water. When the fire burns down, the hot stones are covered with seaweed (the best is rockweed, the kind with little rubbery air puffs, but other kinds also have a good sea-salty flavor). All the food is piled in wire-bottomed steamer boxes placed on the seaweed, and then covered with more seaweed and tarpaulins. Just when you think you can't wait another minute, when the air is fragrant as the sea, the treasure chests are opened and the feast is on.

The best smoked fish I ever had was of Italian descent. That is to say, two great Italian fishermen, John Ghio and Tony Margie, have perfected the art in their jerry-built smokehouse in Stockton, California. They found some decrepit catfish racks sitting on a levy in the California delta, converted an old refrigerator into a smoker, built a firebox tunnel from a grease drum, and went fishing. In the meantime, the garlic in the backyard grew, the herbs and the bay laurel tree flourished, the olive oil arrived from Italy. The resulting shad, perfected over the years, is astonishing.

It has something to do with the green willow for the smoke, the oak for the mellow flavor, the flavors of Italy, and, most of all, the artistry of my friends John and Tony. Since there is no duplicating their method, and this is not a cold-smoke book, here's a reasonable facsimile you can do in your smoke oven or on the grill. John's lovely wife, Angie, has made some polenta to go with the shad.

SMOKED ITALIAN SHAD

6 fillets of shad or other fish, 1 inch thick
1/4 cup olive oil
1 clove garlic, crushed
2 tablespoons chopped mixed fresh herbs
    (rosemary, basil, coriander, parsley)
Salt and freshly ground pepper

Marinate shad in mixture of oil and herbs. Arrange in hinged grill and cook over willow smoke and coals about 4 minutes to a side until fish flakes, basting with marinade. Season with salt and pepper.
Makes 6 servings

ANGIE'S POLENTA

6 cups salted water
1-1/2 cups yellow cornmeal (preferably cornmeal
    marked polenta in Italian markets)
6 green onions, tops only, chopped 1/4 inch thick
1 tablespoon olive oil
3 tablespoons butter
1/2 cup freshly grated Parmesan cheese
1/2 pound natural cream cheese or teleme
    cheese, cut into 6 to 8 thick slices

Bring water to a boil and gradually stir in the cornmeal. Gently simmer, stirring frequently (use long-handled wooden spoon to prevent sticking), for about 45 minutes, or until mixture is very thick. Taste for salt.

While cornmeal is cooking, slowly sauté onion in the olive oil and 2 tablespoons of the butter. Spoon half of the cornmeal mixture onto a serving platter and top with 3 or 4 pieces of the cream cheese, which have been dipped in the Parmesan cheese to coat. Sprinkle with half of the sautéed onions. Repeat layers, ending with the cheese and onions. Top with the remaining tablespoon of butter cut into small bits. Serve immediately.
Makes 6 servings

I've had the pleasure of his company and his magnificent photographs ever since I came out west. His name is Halberstadt and he is known with great affection as Hal. His salmon, grilled over the coals at his misty, sea-salty digs in Bodega Bay, is the best I've ever tasted. "Nothing on it, nothing in it, nothing to it," says he.

HAL'S INCOMPARABLE BODEGA BAY SALMON

Get your salmon *fresh* from icy waters, bright of eye and "firmly convinced." A 6- to 8-pound salmon, called a precocious "half-pounder" by fishermen, is easy to manage on a fairly small grill. Set him on a platter with a little olive oil drizzled on it so he won't stick to the grill. When there is a thick ash on the coals, cook on grill until the flesh begins to go gray, then flip him over gently and cook the other side. Hal says the fish is done when: it feels springy to the touch rather than squashy; the juices begin to surface a milky gray; there is no trace of reddish color in the cavity; and you slit the skin along the back and can just lift the flesh from the bone. (The sweetest end, in case you're given a choice, is the tail.)
Makes 6 servings, if you're lucky

Even today in the Pacific Northwest, on the small islands making up the straits and archipelago of Puget Sound, one can partake in an old Indian celebration—the great salmon fry. Over great stone firepits, roaring to perfection, plump fillets of fresh salmon on thin willow-reed grills are cooked to a succulent deliciousness.

When a "brides' ship" weighed anchor in Jamestown Harbor in 1619 with gay and courageous women on board, no less than 400 feverish bachelors awaited them. Even in the crude log cabins of the settlement, these early Virginians had style. The "brides" had brought their hope chests with wineglasses, two-tined forks, and table knives, pewter dishes and candlesticks. They dined by candlelight on wild turkey. This king of American game birds has been restocked in many states and is a great challenge to hunters.

WILD TURKEY OR TAME, WITH CHESTNUT AND PINE NUT STUFFING

15- to 20-pound turkey with giblets
Salt and freshly ground pepper
1/2 pound unsalted butter
1 cup dry white wine
Several sprigs rosemary
Hickory chips for fuel

Stuffing
1/4 pound unsalted butter
1 clove garlic, crushed
1-1/2 cups bread cubes
2 shallots, minced
2 stalks celery, diced
1 teaspoon chopped fresh rosemary
1/2 teaspoon salt
1/4 teaspoon freshly ground pepper
1/2 cup chopped parsley
1/2 cup chicken stock
2 pinches fresh thyme leaves
2 tablespoons dry sherry

1/2 cup heavy cream
1 cup pine nuts (or any flavorsome nuts)
3/4 pound chestnuts, roasted over the coals, page 32, peeled, and coarsely chopped

To prepare the stuffing, melt the butter in a medium-sized skillet and add the garlic. Cook until lightly golden and then sauté the bread cubes, stirring carefully until they are browned. Remove the bread cubes with a slotted spoon and drain on paper toweling. To the butter in the skillet, add the shallots, celery, rosemary, salt, pepper, parsley, chicken stock, thyme, sherry, and cream. Simmer over low heat for 2 minutes, stirring constantly. Add the browned bread cubes, pine nuts, and chopped chestnuts. Adjust seasonings.

Rub the inside of the turkey with salt and pepper, stuff it with the dressing, and truss the opening. Leave legs untied. Rub the entire turkey with butter, then place the remaining butter in a saucepan with the wine and rosemary sprigs. Bring to a quick boil and remove from heat; use as a basting sauce. Skewer the giblets so that they can be cooked along with the bird.

Balance the turkey on a spit or set in a smoke oven. Place drip pan under bird. Scatter hickory chips over the coals. Basting turkey occasionally with basting sauce, cook 2 to 4 hours, depending on the size of the bird; the meat thermometer should register about 175°F when turkey is done. Add giblets the last hour of cooking. Remove turkey from spit or smoke oven; lift out drip pan. Use drippings for making gravy with the chopped giblets.
Makes 12 to 16 servings

SPLIT BABY TURKEY WITH TARRAGON

6- to 8-pound turkey, split
Juice of 1 lemon
1/4 pound butter
1/2 cup dry white wine
2 cloves garlic, crushed
1/4 cup chopped fresh tarragon

Rub the turkey halves with lemon juice. In a small pan placed on the grill, melt butter and add rest of ingredients. Use this to baste the turkey during cooking. Set turkey on grill and cook over coals about 50 to 60 minutes, turning until nicely charred and tender and basting frequently.
Makes 4 to 6 servings

CHARCOAL-GRILLED TOM TURKEY STEAKS

1 large tom turkey, frozen
1 cup corn or other vegetable oil
1 cup dry white wine
A good pinch crumbled dried sage or poultry
  seasoning
Salt and freshly ground pepper

If you have a good, cooperative butcher, ask him to slice the frozen turkey with his power meat saw into 1-inch-thick steaks, concentrating on the breast meat. Save the dark meat for another day. Marinate the steaks in a mixture of the oil, wine, sage, and salt and pepper 3 or 4 hours at room temperature. Grill over coals about 5 minutes to a side, basting with marinade.
Makes 12 servings

A "tin kitchen" is an old tin oven used on top of early ranges and outside over the campfires. If you ever happen upon one, you can convert it to a smoke oven. I couldn't resist this recipe from an old cookbook that calls for stuffing the bird before he's done in and after.

TIN KITCHEN TURKEY

"Get your turkey six weeks before you need it; put him in a coop just large enough to let him walk, or in a small yard. Give him walnuts—one the first day, and increase every day one till he has 9; then go back to one and up to 9 until you kill him, stuffing him twice with cornmeal dough each day, in which put a little chopped onion and celery, if you have it. For the dressing, use bread, picked up fine, a tablespoonful of butter, some sage, thyme, chopped onion, pepper, salt, and the yolks of two eggs, and pour in a little boiling water to make it stick together; before putting it in the turkey pour boiling water inside and outside, to cleanse and plump it; then roast it in a tin kitchen, basting all the time. It will be splendid, served with a nice piece of ham and cranberry sauce."

A mystical excursion through the wine country outside San Francisco Bay might lead to Paul Drymalski's natural world high on a hill over-looking a chiaroscuro of Napa Valley vineyards. Paul has harnessed the sun, the water, the good earth and, it seems to me, the very air. His *poulet fumé* is one of his own Rhode Island reds, apple-smoked and tasting faintly of the fresh wild blue-berries that grow around the farm. His succulent and surprising stuffing has the texture of a good pâté and is made from a recycled tough old bird. Paul makes the noodles for the fettuccine, he plucks a ripe tomato from the vine to toss with fresh sweet basil and elephant garlic for the sauce, he picks ripe figs and plums for tarts—and he sauces his guests generously with his warmth and wine.

PAUL'S APPLE-SMOKED POULET FUMÉ
With a Stuffing of Recycled Tough Old Bird

3-1/2- to 5-pound roasting chicken
1 tough old bird (a stewing hen)
1/2 cup dried mushrooms, soaked in hot water
   and drained
2 cloves garlic, minced
1/4 cup dry sherry
1 egg, lightly beaten
1-1/2 teaspoons salt
Chopped fresh parsley, thyme, and sage to taste
A splash of cognac
Apple wood chips for fuel

Rinse roasting chicken, pat dry, and pull out fat from cavity. Do the same with the other chicken. With a boning knife, cut flesh from breast and thighs of the tough bird and grind finely with the chicken fat in your food processor or meat grinder. Mix lightly with rest of ingredients. Mixture should be soft, but not runny. (You can add bread crumbs if it's too soft.) Fill cavity of chicken with stuffing and truss bird. Set in a smoke oven fired with apple wood chips. Cook very slowly 3 to 4 hours, or until meat thermometer registers 170°F.
Makes 4 servings

In ancient Rome and Greece, the master of the house was the master of the *furnus,* where all the serious cooking took place. At the elegant Stanford Court Hotel in San Francisco, the master of the house, Jim Nassikas, has created a uniquely theatrical dining experience in his Fournou's Ovens. Patterned after the famous fifteenth-century Casa Botin in Madrid, where the coals in the ovens were kept perpetually glowing for over 200 years, the roasts and racks are fed into a 35-square-foot, oak-fired oven, an "amphitheater" in clear view—and indeed, clear smell—of the diners.

ROAST NATIVE DUCKLING WITH GREEN PEPPERCORN AND KUMQUAT SAUCE

3 ducks, 4 to 5 pounds each
1 large onion, coarsely chopped
2 stalks celery, cut into 1-inch slices
6 carrots, peeled and sliced
Salt and freshly ground pepper
1 quart box fresh kumquats
1/4 cup white vinegar
1 cup each sugar and fresh orange juice
1/4 cup fresh lemon juice
1/2 teaspoon crushed black peppercorns
1 bay leaf
1 small sprig thyme
1 small leek, thinly sliced
2 cups demi-glace (brown sauce)
1/2 cup tomato paste
1/4 cup Cointreau or Grand Marnier
3 tablespoons green peppercorns, well drained

Wash ducks and pat dry. Divide onion, celery, and carrots in thirds and fill each duck cavity with the vegetables. Sprinkle with salt and pepper. Set ducks in a smoke oven and roast for about 1-1/2 to 2 hours, or until a meat thermometer reaches 170°F.

While ducks are roasting, make the sauce. Peel half of the kumquats, removing all pulp from peel (reserve pulp). Cut peels in fine julienne, cover with boiling water for 1 minute, drain, and reserve. In a saucepan over medium heat, cook vinegar and sugar until it begins to caramelize. Add citrus juices and the pulp from peeled kumquats. Cook until liquid reduces by about one-fourth. Add the kumquat peel julienne, crushed peppercorns, bay leaf, thyme, and leek. Simmer until golden brown. Then add the demi-glace and tomato paste. Simmer, stirring occasionally, 1 hour. Strain through a fine sieve and add the liqueur and green peppercorns. Halve ducks and arrange on heated platters. Garnish with remaining kumquats cut in thin slices. Reheat sauce and serve separately.
Makes 6 to 8 servings

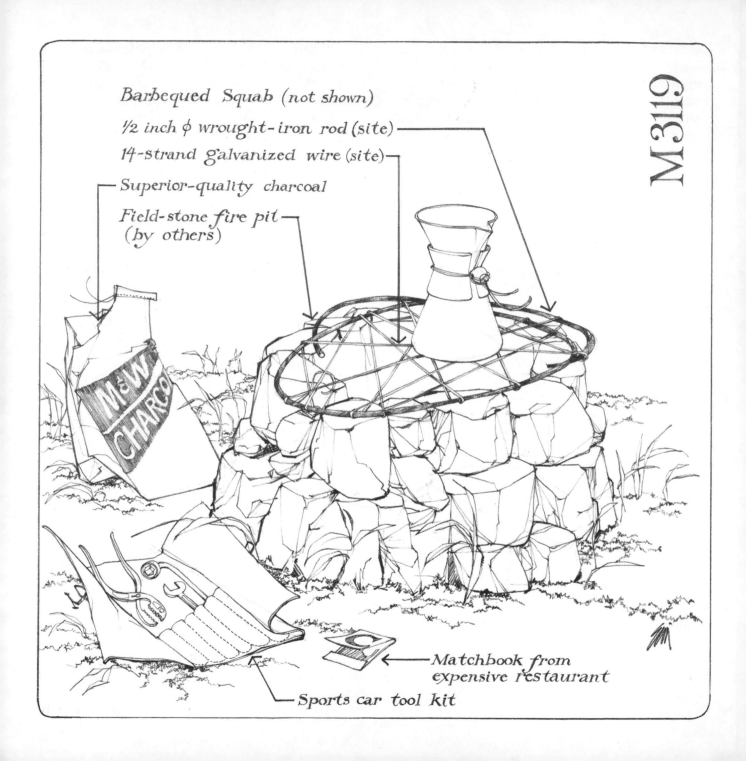

Barbequed Squab (not shown)

½ inch φ wrought-iron rod (site)

14-strand galvanized wire (site)

Superior-quality charcoal

Field-stone fire pit
(by others)

M 319

Matchbook from
expensive restaurant

Sports car tool kit

The chuck wagon cook, called "cookie" or "coosie" (from the Spanish name *cocinero*), was absolute boss of the wagon. He was also generally a despot, whose cussedness inspired the old saw: "Only a fool argues with a skunk, a mule, or a cook."

The camp chow was cooked over open fires in trenches or pits to hold the heat. When wood was in short supply or non-existent, as in much of the Southwest, the cook used "prairie coal" or cow manure, which burns well when dry. Cookie rewarded the cowboys when they brought in a gunny sackful.

COOSIE'S DRUNKEN MUTTON OR LAMB

1 large leg of mutton (or use lamb if you prefer)

Salsa Borracha with Tequila
4 dried pasilla chili peppers
1-1/2 cups water
2 cloves garlic
1/2 cup olive oil
1 large onion, cut into chunks
2 pickled serrano chili peppers
2 ounces dry cheese (dry Monterey Jack or
   Parmesan will do), grated
1/2 cup tequila
2 teaspoons salt
1 tablespoon red wine vinegar

Balance meat on a spit and roast over coals until done to your liking (1-1/2 to 2-1/2 hours).

While mutton is roasting, prepare sauce. Parch the pasilla chilies in a ungreased heavy skillet placed on the grill for a few minutes, turning so that they will not burn. Remove stems and seeds and cover the pods with the water. In about 1 hour, put pods in a blender with the remaining ingredients and 1/2 cup of the soaking water. Blend until smooth, adding remaining soaking water. I have purposely made the sauce mild. If you wish, you may add 3 or 4 more serrano chili peppers for extra heat. Carve the leg of mutton and serve with the Salsa Borracha on the side. *Frijoles refritos* make a nice accompaniment.
Makes 6 to 8 servings

A Mark Twain-type Americana on camping . . .
"You remember the silver, pack the crystal and coffeemaker, trim the candles, but forget the grill." Early California outdoor charcoal stove, Cree Ranch, Turlock, The Valley, circa 1962

My good friends Peg and Paul Rusche live just below Yosemite in Mariposa, where they have built a warm and earthy home arbored with grapes. The pantry is always full of home-grown, home-canned, or sun-dried marvels. This is for when the recipe calls for one tablespoon of tomato paste.

COOKING WITH THE PRIMAL FIRE

"Wait for a hot, dry spell, 98° to 100°F. Take 20 tomatoes, nice ripe ones, and chop them, leaving skins on but removing about half the seeds. (You could leave the seeds in entirely but they make a bitter flavor if there are too many.) Chop a couple of onions, 2 cloves of garlic, and a few hot peppers, if you like. Other seasonings can be added, but do not add salt! Add 1 to 2 tablespoons of sugar, just enough to cut the bitter acid flavor a bit. Cook all ingredients for about 10 minutes, then purée in blender.

"Line 5 jelly-roll pans or rimmed cookie sheets with heavy plastic. Do this carefully so that the tomato mixture, which is very watery, will not run out onto the metal. Fill pans with purée about 3/8 inch thick. Put in the sun for 2 to 3 days, depending on the climate. Bring the trays inside if the nights are damp. When tomato mixture is dry to the flexible leather stage, peel off plastic and continue drying to brittle stage. (You can eat this as tomato leather if you like.) When thoroughly dry and brittle, crack up into small pieces and powder in the blender. You will end up with about 2 cups of powder. Store in a covered glass jar in a dry place; dark, too. Half a tablespoon of powder more or less equals a tablespoon of paste. Very convenient. You can also make barbecue sauce, a nice cup of soup, or use it in stews, etc."

SKEWERED LAMB LIVER WITH BREAD AND BACON AND PRIMAL FIRE

1 pound lamb liver, thinly sliced
Primal Fire, preceding
1 cup fresh basil leaves
French bread cubes
Blanched bacon strips

Cut liver slices in strips about 1-1/2 inches wide. Dust with Primal Fire. Lay a few basil leaves on each strip, roll up, and string on skewers alternately with cubes of bread about the same size. Wrap liver and bread with strips of bacon. Set on grill and cook, turning, until bacon is crisp.
Makes 4 servings

Istanbul was once the cosmopolis of the world—a mecca for Turks, Greeks, Arabs, Syrians, Armenians, Circassians, Bulgars, Jews, Genoese, and Florentines. Each was part of the exotic blend that made up the cuisine of Turkey. Carl Chooljian of the California Raisin Advisory Board is my Middle Eastern connection in Fresno. His reputation as a cook is formidable, his simple kabobs, perfection, even for as many as the 300 people at his annual holiday "office party." He has his butcher bone a leg of lamb and remove the gristle and fat. He then uses only the upper portion for the kabobs, and serves them with a pilaf studded with raisins.

CARL CHOOLJIAN'S ARMENIAN SHISH KEBABS

3 pounds boneless leg of lamb, cut into 1-1/2-inch cubes
2 red onions, thickly sliced
1/4 cup dry red wine
Olive oil
1 green bell pepper, cut into squares (optional)
2 tablespoons seasoned salt (use a commercial blend or your own concoction)
1 teaspoon freshly ground pepper
1/2 teaspoon paprika

Toss lamb cubes with onions, wine, and enough oil to just coat. Marinate 4 hours or overnight in the refrigerator. Thread meat on skewers, alternating cubes with onions and bell pepper, if desired. Sprinkle with seasoned salt, pepper, and paprika. Grill quickly on all sides over coals until beautifully brown but still pink and juicy.
Makes 6 servings

At the International Exposition in St. Louis in 1904, the greatest culinary invention in America came to be—the hamburger on a bun. A little hamburger stand across the street from the unemployment office in San Francisco illustrates the ethnic assimilation of the burger by the condiments on the "serving" table: Mexican hot chili sauce, Chinese soy sauce, Japanese teriyaki sauce, German mustard, Heinz ketchup, piccalilli . . . and marmalade (English?).

My favorite hamburgers are lightly shaped around a little ice cube to keep them moist.

SAN FRANCISCO HAMBURGERS

1-1/2 pounds lean ground beef
Coarse salt and pepper
1 cup good burgundy
4 tablespoons butter
1 cup finely chopped fresh herbs (parsley, green onions, or whatever happens to be available)
1/4 cup Chinese oyster sauce (available in Oriental markets and some supermarkets)
4 thick slices sourdough French bread

Lightly season the meat with salt and pepper. Shape into 4 large patties around 4 little ice cubes. Put on the grill and cook until nicely charred, rare and juicy, turning once. This should take about 8 to 10 minutes. Meanwhile, in a small saucepan combine wine, butter, and herbs and reduce to about half. Add oyster sauce and mix well. Pour over hamburgers set on thick slices of bread.
Makes 4 servings

In spite of the many tender words given to various cuts of steak, the best ones come from the short loin. The porterhouse and T-bone are used interchangeably, varying with the amount of fillet and "tail." The club comes from the small end next to the rib and has no tenderloin, unlike the fancy steaks variously dubbed *filet mignon, tournedos, Chateaubriand* (and this is more of a recipe than a cut, says *Larousse Gastronomique*). It may be a bit confusing that the top loin becomes a New York strip in Kansas City and just the opposite in New York, but it's all a matter of what language your butcher speaks. The sirloin is just aft of the short loin and not quite as tender, but still excellent for charcoal grilling, as are the rib steaks that the French call *entrecôtes*.

Here's the inside information on a couple of inside steaks from Merle Ellis, my favorite butcher. The "skirt," which is actually the diaphragm muscle, is great for charcoal-grilling because it has a light coat of fat that bastes the meat as it cooks. The "hanging tender" hangs from the kidney just below the tenderloin and is known in the trade as the butcher's steak because there's just one to an animal and the butcher gets first grabs.

GARLIC STEAK AND SPUDS

8 small potatoes, barely cooked through
2 skirt steaks
6 cloves garlic, crushed
1/4 cup olive oil
1 large onion, cut up
1 cup red wine
2 tablespoons soy sauce
Chopped parsley

Pierce potatoes with fork. Marinate steak and potatoes in rest of ingredients for 1 hour or so at room temperature. Thread on skewers. Grill steaks and potatoes over coals, basting with marinade, to desired doneness.
Makes 4 servings

THE HANGING TENDERLOIN

1 hanging tenderloin, about 2 pounds
1/4 cup each olive oil and red wine
2 cloves garlic, minced or crushed
1 teaspoon crumbled dried oregano
Salt and freshly ground pepper

Marinate steak in all remaining ingredients for an hour or so. Grill over coals, turning only once, to desired doneness. Slice across the grain, on the diagonal from top to the bottom of the steak.
Makes 4 or 6 servings

On the menu at the Bear Hollow Restaurant on Castro Street in San Francisco: Bear Hollow Steak —their own special cut charbroiled to your likeness.

SALT-ROASTED STEAK

3 pounds (7-1/2 cups) coarse-medium salt
2 pounds beef tenderloin, in 1 piece
1/4 pound butter or margarine
2 cloves garlic, minced
1 loaf French bread, cut in 1/2-inch-thick slices
    and toasted on one side

Mix just enough water (about 2-1/4 cups) with the salt to make it like damp sand. In a hinged grill, place a double thickness of paper towels, about the size of the meat. Pat out half the salt on the towels; top with meat. Completely cover meat with remaining salt, coating evenly (this keeps the juices in). Now cover with a double thickness of paper toweling, overlapping the edges (don't worry, only the towel edges will burn). Close grill. Grill close to coals 12 to 15 minutes per side. Crack off hardened cakes of salt, scraping off any that clings. Thinly slice meat. Melt butter in a skillet and add garlic. Dip untoasted side of bread in garlic butter and top with slices of meat.
Makes 8 servings

Around the corner from my cottage on Russian Hill in San Francisco is a choice French butcher shop run by Henri Lapuyade. I've marveled at the artistry and charm of Pierre Allain who holds court there. Right out of a Parisian school, he took first prize in a professional competition among butchers and headed shortly thereafter for America. When I asked him how he became such a master, he allowed as how his first job required him to custom-tailor cuts of meat to those little bitty trays for airlines. *Alors!*

PIERRE ALLAIN'S
"BEST AND PREFERRED BARBECUE"

"I prefer a chuck roast or chuck steak so well aged it's practically brown. I marinate it in a mixture of Kikkoman, garlic powder, salt, and black pepper.

"I have a barbecue with a wall halfway in the back. Once the coals are hot, I push them around the wall. I make a special bracket for the grill at a 45-degree angle so that the fat doesn't drop on the coals and burn, which gives a bad taste to the meat. The other secret is to keep watching and turning, taking care that it doesn't burn. You can serve it in chunks or slice it. Hardly any salt is needed, since the Kikkoman seasons the meat."

This is the story of Henry Ford and his Model T briquette. In 1924, Henry built a plant near the hardwood forests in Wisconsin to make wood parts for his Model T. The wooden scrap piled up, so he had to build another plant to burn it, thus creating a charcoal plant. Henry had the notion to improve the quality and reduce the shipping bulk by developing the briquette. The charcoal plant became so productive that industry couldn't absorb all the briquettes, so Henry had the notion to sell them to the public for outdoor cooking. He foisted bags of briquettes on the doorsteps of his Ford dealers but, alas, Henry's cookout didn't catch on (much to the relief of the dealers) until the Kingsford Company acquired the plant. John Whetton of the Kingsford Company told me this fascinating tale and he also told me a lot about the Charcoal Barbecue Industry of which he is President. John and his wife have three youngsters and four barbecues, which would seem to indicate that cooking is this family's favorite outdoor sport.

The truth is, you don't really need a cooker at all when you use quality charcoal that produces a fine ash—just brush it off and toss your steaks right on the coals. For sheer showmanship, there's nothing like it.

CHARRED RIGHT ON THE COALS MODEL T STEAKS

Have your steaks cut about 2 inches thick; rub them with garlic and olive oil and let stand while you build up your glowing coals to a depth of about 3 inches. When they're ashy gray, brush them off. Toss your steaks right on the coals—they won't burn, they just damp down the fire a bit (unless your coals are too deep and too hot). In 5 minutes or so, flip them over to coals that haven't been covered before and continue cooking them another 5 minutes, adding some herbs to the coals and brushing steaks with a bit of oil.

Quite by accident, Mr. H. F. Ford discovered a source of readily available charcoal . . . the hardwood briquette.

Don Jackson, currently Chairman of the California Beef Council, described a most memorable cookout when he was buying cattle south of Nogales. A Mexican cowhand had rigged a primitive dome out of bent re-bars, which he then laced with heavy barbed wire. Hanging from a nearby tree was a huge haunch of beef that he deftly cut into thin overlapping slices, "like a big sheet of cookies." When the coal and mesquite fire was just right, he draped the sheet of steaks over the dome, charred it quickly, and flipped it over on the other side.

THE JACKSONS' WHOLE FRENCH FILLET

1 whole beef fillet
1/4 cup peppercorns, crushed
1/3 cup cognac or brandy, warmed in a small
  pan placed on the grill
1 cup heavy cream
2 tablespoons French-style mustard
1 tablespoon Worcestershire sauce
Juice of 1/4 lemon

Press crushed peppercorns into the fillet. Grill over coals, turning once. Fillet will be done when meat thermometer registers 120°F. When done, brush off excess pepper and immediately place meat on a heated platter; pour over the cognac and flame.

While the meat is cooking, bring to a gentle boil the cream, mustard, and Worcestershire sauce, stirring constantly for 3 minutes to thicken slightly. Stir in lemon juice and remove from heat.

Carve the fillet, making 3 thin slices for each serving. Add the juices from carving to the sauce and pour the sauce over each serving.
Makes 8 or more servings

"Carnival" means literally "farewell to meat," a Latin derivation. *Mardi Gras* is French for "fat Tuesday." Altogether, the three words describe the festive New Orleans hullabaloo that precedes the rigors of Lent. Live and feast today, for tomorrow you fast. Every Acadian cookout is well peppered with Tabasco, the sauce that has seared tongues from here to Hong Kong.

MIXED GRILL
EN BROCHETTES "GARGANTUA"
Giant Mixed Grill on Long Skewers

1 pound lean pork, cut from the loin
1 pound fillet of beef, cut from the tail end
1 pound lean lamb, cut from the loin
6 thick slices bacon
2 green bell peppers
2 onions, cut into very thin slices
8 bay leaves, cut in half
Salt and freshly ground black pepper
A few pinches each fresh thyme and oregano

Marinade
1 cup olive oil (a mild one is best)
1/2 teaspoon Tabasco sauce
2 sprigs thyme, or
1/2 teaspoon crumbled dried thyme
2 bay leaves
1 sprig rosemary, or
1/4 teaspoon crumbled dried rosemary
Cracked peppercorns

Cut the meats, bacon, and green peppers into the size of butter pats. Thread meats, vegetables, and bay leaves as follows onto 4 long skewers. For each: 1 slice green pepper, 1 slice beef, 1 slice onion, 1 slice veal, 1 slice green pepper, 1 slice bacon, 1/2 bay leaf, 1 slice lamb, 1 slice bacon, and 1 slice onion. Push the meats close together.

Combine all the ingredients for the marinade and carefully coat the skewered meat and vegetables with it, using a brush. Let stand 15 to 20 minutes on a rack, allowing the excess oil to drain. Sprinkle with salt and pepper and a few pinches of thyme and oregano. Cook over coals, allowing to brown nicely on all sides.
Makes 4 servings

The word *criollo,* which means "children of colonists," is the origin of the name *Creole.* Judah Jones grills Creole style in a big way on a big rig that he hauls around from place to place in the backwoods of California. He plies you with both pork and beef ribs, snapper, and chicken, and he daintily passes out warm moist towels for mopping up.

JUDAH'S CREOLE MIXED GRILL

3 to 4 pounds pork or beef ribs, in 1 piece
2 pounds large shrimp in the shell, deveined
1 cup Louisiana Smoky Sauce, following
2 pounds chicken drumsticks with thighs
Corn oil
Salt and freshly ground pepper
2 whole dressed red snappers (3 to 4 pounds each)
1/2 cup chopped onion
6 lemon slices
Louisiana Smoky Sauce for basting
1/4 cup dry sherry

Simmer ribs in water to cover until partially cooked, about 30 to 40 minutes. Drain and pat dry. Set shrimp on a large rectangle of heavy foil, pour the 1 cup Louisiana Smoky Sauce over them, and fold up foil securely. Marinate 1 to 2 hours. Brush chicken pieces with corn oil and sprinkle with salt and pepper. Rinse and pat dry the snappers and rub skin with corn oil. Sprinkle with salt and pepper and tuck into each cavity half of the onions and lemon slices.

You'll need a large barbecue with a hood (or heavy foil to cover food on the grill). The meats and seafood should be added to the grill so that they are all finished cooking at about the same time. Place ribs on grill and cook, basting with sauce, until nicely browned, about 45 minutes. Set chicken on the grill and cook, turning, about 15 minutes; then brush with sauce and continue cooking, basting frequently, until nicely browned. Set red snappers and the shrimp packet on grill and cook about 25 minutes, until fish flakes easily. Brush lightly with a little smoky sauce. Remove meats and seafood from grill. Open shrimp packet and sprinkle sherry over shrimp. Serve meats and seafood with extra smoky sauce at the table. Dirty rice—cooked rice with chopped giblets, celery, green pepper, and brown gravy—and hot-water corn cakes make good accompaniments.
Makes 12 to 16 servings

LOUISIANA SMOKY SAUCE

2 cups ketchup
1 cup water
1/2 cup each cider vinegar and sugar
1/2 cup each chopped celery, onion, parsley,
   green bell pepper, and tomato
2 tablespoons Worcestershire sauce
1 tablespoon liquid smoke
1 teaspoon each crumbled dried basil, marjoram,
   and oregano
1 teaspoon ground cinnamon
4 tablespoons butter

Combine all ingredients in a saucepan and cook uncovered over medium heat until reduced to 1 quart, about 30 minutes.
Makes 1 quart

The curious cuisine called "Tex-Mex" is an authentic folk festival in itself. A prestigious Texas friend, who chose to remain anonymous, told me about a typical "black tie" barbecue, always a charity event. You start out with a whole lot of "border buttermilk," tequila and ruby red (grapefruit juice) on the rocks, and you end up likewise. In between you have the cockroach race, the wet T-shirt competition, the watermelon seed spit, the kicker-dancing. And then you have perfectly barbecued beef brisket and ribs, spicy beans in a homemade chili sauce, fresh hot biscuits, and lots of melted butter in your own tin cup to brush on the roastin' corn. "And *always* those damned fried apple pies and chocolate chip cookies in plastic bags." (Get some mugwort to throw on the fire after the barbecue to ward off the mosquitos.)

TEXAS "BLACK TIE" SHORTRIBS

5 pounds lean, meaty beef short ribs
1/4 cup Homemade Chili Powder, following
2 cups dry red wine
1/2 cup olive or peanut oil
2 large onions, chopped
4 cloves garlic, crushed
Salt and freshly ground pepper to taste
1 bay leaf
1/4 to 1/2 cup Homemade Chili Sauce, following

Spread out ribs in a shallow pan. Rub with chili powder and let stand an hour or so. Cover with a mixture of rest of ingredients and let stand at least 4 hours. Drain off marinade and save for basting. Set meat on grill over coals, or preferably in a smoke oven, and baste often with marinade as it cooks. After about 40 to 50 minutes cooking, the meat will be richly browned and pink inside.
Makes 8 to 10 servings

HOMEMADE CHILI POWDER

1/4 cup dried chili peppers (use mild ones, such as Anaheim or pasilla, or a combination of mild and hot)
1 tablespoon cumin seeds
2 teaspoons salt
1 teaspoon each ground cloves and coriander

In a blender whirl chili peppers and cumin seeds to a powder. Mix well with rest of ingredients. Store in airtight container.
Makes approximately 1/4 cup

HOMEMADE CHILI SAUCE

16 dried Anaheim or pasilla chili peppers
1/4 cup peanut oil
2 large onions, chopped
4 cloves garlic, chopped
2-1/2 cups water
Salt and freshly ground pepper
Sugar

Remove stems and seeds of chili peppers and whirl pods in a blender until they form a powder. Heat the oil in a saucepan and cook the onions and garlic until translucent. Add ground chili peppers and water and simmer, uncovered, 5 minutes. Season to taste with salt, pepper, and sugar. Store in the refrigerator in a jar with a tight-fitting lid.
Makes approximately 2-1/2 cups

Constantine the Great, Emperor of Rome, decided sausage was too good for the hoi polloi and banned it, thus creating sausage speakeasies from here to the Forum. Those days have passed, but the sausage lives on and on—on everything from the good Frau Feuchtwanger's original St. Louis hot dog bun to tortillas, peda bread, pizza dough, and, irreverently, wrapped up in a *croissant*.

HOT DOGS I HAVE KNOWN AND LOVED

All-American Yankee Frank These old-fashioned kind in real skins or casings, all beef, preferably kosher from Chicago. With a crusty roll toasted on the grill, that daffodil-yellow mustard (which I otherwise disdain), some good homemade piccalilli.

Mexican Grilled hot dog, hot black beans, shredded cheese, and lettuce, cool/hot green chili sauce, tomato relish, guacamole on a warm tortilla.

German Sauerkraut and Münster cheese, hot German mustard, a good rye roll or bread, buttered and grilled along with the hot dog, knockwurst, bratwurst, or whatever.

French Mayonnaise, of course, chopped herbs, a thin slice of good ham, and maybe some brie, all done up in a French roll with a grilled *chien*!

Middle Eastern A kabob of a dog, cut in thirds and skewered with thick onion wedges, green or red bell pepper squares, eggplant chunks. When nicely charred, fold it up in peda bread and slip the whole meal off the skewer.

Italian Sweet with anise or hot with pepper, Italian sausages are best poached 5 to 8 minutes before grilling. Serve in crusty Italian rolls with an eggplant relish called *caponata*, available in jars.

Social notes from the Weekly Register of May 24, 1917: "Last Saturday, Mrs. Clarrise Malcolm-Witherbottom transported her entire entourage to one of the outlying airdromes to hold an after-the-hunt brunch for our young lads who will bravely patrol the skies. Out of patriotic deference to these times of peril, hot dogs were served."

While it may seem troublesome to separate the nut from its spiny covering, the delicious flavor of the chestnut makes the reward worth the work. Grill up a bunch for adding to a stuffing for fowl or to serve friends after a charcoal-grilled feast.

ROASTED CHESTNUTS

Make an X with a sharp knife on the flat side of each chestnut. Place the chestnuts in a shallow pan and set on the grill over the coals. Roast until the skin begins to lift away from the nut and the air becomes fragrant with their smell. Peel them while they are still hot or the inner brown skin will not come off easily.

The argument continues over why the Indians called hard spirits "fire water." The truth is, it burns a blue flame when you spit it into an open fire. It also burns a blue flame when you warm it gently and flame it over steak. The butcher shops in California's Gold Country, including Mr. Armour's fancy establishment, were more apt to have grizzly and venison steaks than any other. The grand old Palace Hotel in San Francisco featured a smoked leg of venison with a marinade that both tamed the game and gave a kick to the lovely chestnut sauce.

THE OLD PALACE'S LEG OF VENISON
With a Roasted Chestnut Sauce

1 leg of venison or lamb
6 slices fat bacon

Marinade
1 fifth burgundy
1 large onion, sliced
1 clove garlic, crushed
1 bay leaf
3 juniper berries, crushed

Chestnut Sauce
1 pound mushrooms, sliced
1/4 pound butter
1/4 cup flour
1 cup beef or chicken stock
1-1/2 cups sour cream
1 pound chestnuts, roasted over the coals,
    preceding, peeled, and coarsely chopped
Salt and freshly ground pepper

Combine all ingredients for the marinade and marinate venison several hours or overnight. With a larding needle, lard venison with bacon slices. Balance meat on a spit or set in a smoke oven and cook, basting frequently with marinade (save rest for sauce), until meat thermometer registers 135° to 145°F for medium rare, approximately 1-1/2 to 2 hours. While meat cooks, make the sauce.

Sauté mushrooms in butter until soft; add flour gradually and stir until smooth. Add the stock and 1 cup of the marinade, which has been strained. As soon as sauce thickens, add sour cream and chestnuts and stir until well blended. Do not allow sauce to boil. It should be the consistency of heavy cream; thin, if necessary, with a little stock. Season to taste with salt and pepper. Pour into a bowl and serve with venison.
Makes 6 servings

VENISON GRILLED HASH FOR BREAKFAST

1 pound ground venison
1 tart green apple, cored and chopped
1 green bell pepper, chopped
2 tablespoons raisins, chopped
A good squeeze of lemon juice
1/2 teaspoon salt
1/4 teaspoon freshly ground pepper
Peanut oil

Combine all ingredients except oil and shape into 4 patties. Brush with oil and cook in hinged grill over coals.
Makes 4 servings

VENISON HAMBURGERS

1 pound ground venison
1 tablespoon chopped onion
1 tablespoon each olive oil and dry red wine
1/2 teaspoon salt
1/4 teaspoon freshly ground pepper
Olive oil

Combine all ingredients and shape into 3 or 4 patties. Cook in hinged grill over coals, brushing with olive oil if desired.
Makes 3 or 4 servings

THE CELLARMASTER'S MARINADES AND BASTING SAUCES

Vitis vinifera, the noble wine grape, came to California with the Spaniards via Mexico—perhaps in the baggage of the Franciscan padre Junipero Serra. The first to produce quality wine was the *commandante general* of the Mexican army, Mariano Guadalupe Vallejo, at Sonoma, and a little later his friendly rival, Colonel Agoston Haraszthy, an expatriate Hungarian. For many years I have worked with The Christian Brothers and their wise and witty cellarmaster, Brother Timothy, in the Napa Valley. I have developed many recipes for their wine promotions, including some favorite basting sauces and marinades with their wines. And I like to use little brooms of rosemary, parsley, and bay for my brushes, varying them with the seasons and the supply.

FOR VEAL AND CHICKEN

1 cup The Christian Brothers Napa Rosé
1 teaspoon each crumbled dried rosemary
    and chervil
Pinch of grated ginger root
Grated zest and juice of 1 lemon
4 tablespoons butter

Set a small saucepan with the rosé, rosemary, chervil, ginger root, grated zest, and juice on the side of the grill. Let simmer about 10 minutes. Remove from the fire and add the butter, a spoonful at a time, until it melts and sauce is slightly thickened. Use to baste veal and chicken as it cooks.
Makes approximately 1 cup

FOR DUCK

The Christian Brothers Brandy
Salt and freshly ground pepper
1 cup fresh orange juice
3 tablespoons Cointreau
Pinch each grated ginger root and crumbled dried
    tarragon

Rub the duck inside and out with brandy, salt and pepper. Set in a pan and flame with 1/4 cup warmed brandy. Mix together the orange juice, Cointreau, 1/4 cup brandy, ginger root, and tarragon and pour over the duck. Use as a marinade and basting sauce.
Makes approximately 1-1/2 cups

FOR RED MEAT AND GAMY GAME

The Christian Brothers Brandy
2 cups The Christian Brothers Burgundy
Grated zest and juice of 1 orange
Juice of 2 lemons
8 peppercorns, crushed
2 cloves garlic, crushed
1/4 cup red wine vinegar
1/2 cup olive or peanut oil
A little chopped carrot, onion, and celery leaves
A good pinch each crumbled dried thyme and
 oregano and salt
2 bay leaves, crumbled

Rub the meat or game with brandy, set it in a large pan, and flame it with 1/4 cup warmed brandy. Combine rest of ingredients and pour over meat. Let stand 2 hours or longer.
Makes approximately 1 quart

FOR FISH

1 cup The Christian Brothers Pinot Chardonnay
Grated zest and juice of 1 lemon
Approximately 1/4 cup olive or peanut oil
 (amount depends on whether the fish is lean
 or fatty)
Chopped fresh tarragon or crumbled
 dried tarragon
Sea salt to taste

Mix together all ingredients. Pour over fish in shallow dish. Marinate 1 hour or so, turning occasionally. Grill fish, basting with marinade.
Makes approximately 1-1/2 cups

Tom Yoshinaga is an executive with Kikkoman International, a firm famous for the soy and teriyaki sauces so important to the Japanese cuisine— and, indeed, the whole charcoal cooking scene. Tom grew up on a farm in southern California where his fondest memories of open-fire cooking are of the Mexican cowhands who heated their *burritos* stuffed with scrambled eggs and hot chilies over little fires in the fields. A man of eclectic tastes, Tom cooks on an hibachi in a highrise apartment and mixes his favorite basting sauce with a good English lime marmalade.

TOM YOSHINAGA'S LONDON TERIYAKI

In a shaker jar, mix 2 parts Kikkoman Teriyaki Sauce with 1 part good lime marmalade or orange/ pineapple juice concentrate. Use to glaze ribs, steaks, or chicken the last 15 minutes of grilling.

FRESH LEMON MARINADE

Mix 1 cup Kikkoman Teriyaki Sauce with 2 tablespoons grated lemon zest and the juice of 1 lemon. Use as a marinade for fresh salmon, chicken, or other fish steaks or fillets or poultry.

What with the price and quality of most "cold cuts," you'd do well to make your own and smoke them in your smoke oven, the way the early American settlers did. You can vary the taste with herbs and spices, mustard seeds, chili powder, or whatever. The brisket is surprisingly good cooked just to the rare stage, thinly sliced on the diagonal, and served to a hungry mob in the form of sourdough French bread sandwiches. Along with the brisket and homemade salami, you might want to do a tongue (boil it first), or a lamb or pork roast.

SMOKED RARIFIED BRISKET
FOR SOURDOUGH SANDWICHES

4- to 5-pound beef brisket, trimmed of fat
3 cloves garlic, slivered
2 thick slices bacon, chopped
1/4 cup chopped parsley
Paprika, crumbled dried thyme, salt, and
    freshly ground pepper

Cut gashes in meat and poke in a sliver of garlic with a little bacon that has been mixed with the parsley. Dust generously on both sides with paprika, thyme, salt, and pepper. Set in smoke oven and cook 35 to 45 minutes, or until meat thermometer registers 150°F for rare. Slice meat on the diagonal to serve.
Makes 8 servings

The bison provided the Plains Indian more than his food and his clothing. The horns were shaped into utensils, the ribs were made into sled runners, and the hide was converted to rope, shields and teepees.

HOMEMADE SMOKED BEEF OR
VENISON SALAMI

4 pounds ground chuck with fat content no more
    than 15 percent or ground venison
1/4 cup curing salt*
3 tablespoons dry red wine
4 cloves garlic, crushed
1 tablespoon cracked peppercorns

Mix together all ingredients. Chill overnight. Divide into 1-pound rolls about 8 inches long, shaping in coarse nylon netting. Tie ends. Cook slowly in your smoke oven about 2 hours. Cool. Wrap in foil to refrigerate or freeze. Slice thin to serve. Keeps in refrigerator up to 3 weeks or frozen up to 2 months.
Makes 4 pounds

*Curing salt is a mixture of sugar, salt, spices, and a preservative that gives meat an appetizing color. It can be purchased from butchers' equipment and supply companies, feed stores, sausage makers, and salt companies.

My old friend Bob Mercer of The Potato Board would never forgive me if I didn't give equal space to the splendiferous spud. A steak is lonesome without a potato, I always say.

POTATOES, U.S.A.

Salt-roasted Spuds Mix a batch of coarse-medium salt with enough water to make "cement." Rub potatoes with good lard, then pack evenly with salt. Cook right in the coals until tender, about 1 hour. Crack off salt, slash potatoes, and slather on the butter, salt, and pepper.

Rosin Potatoes This is an old-time way of cooking potatoes outdoors—and they always seem to taste better, lighter, and fluffier. Place a large heavy kettle in the coals and melt rosin to a depth of about 6 inches. When it boils, drop in the potatoes and let them bubble away for 20 minutes or so until they're tender. Plop each potato in the center of an old newspaper, wrap it up, and twist the ends. It will keep hot until you're ready for it. Then simply slash through the newspaper and skin and plop on the butter.

Potato Kabobs Boil little round potatoes until they are just barely tender. Rub with lard and roll in crushed red and black pepper with some coarse salt. String on skewers and grill until nicely charred.

Reupholstered Potatoes Bake large potatoes, slash, and scoop out the flesh. Mix lightly with butter, sour cream, chopped green chilies and green onions, salt, and pepper. Refill skins, wrap in foil, and set in the coals until nice and hot. You could add some crumbled bacon, cheese, chorizo, whatever.

Poor Boises Rub some big baking potatoes with lard, salt, and coarse pepper. Toss in the coals and roast until tender, about 1 hour. Meanwhile, grill your fresh-caught mountain trout with some slab bacon, cut thick. Brown a good chunk of unsalted butter in a little saucepan on the side of the grill and cut some lemons in half. Slash the potatoes and flatten out on plates. Top with trout, bacon, brown butter, and lemon juice. Poor Boises, indeed!

Early man discovered that the hard kernel of wild grasses, all but indigestible, could be made into food by cracking its husk in an open fire, thus creating popcorn. And who knows the discoverer of this method for popping corn over the grill?

POPPING POPCORN IN A FLOUR SIFTER

Oil is not necessary in this method. The reason oil is used in popping corn in a pan is that the oil helps heat the corn to the point of popping.

Pour 2 to 3 tablespoons of popcorn in a large flour sifter. Cover the sifter with foil and place on the grill 4 to 8 inches above the coals. Shake the sifter back and forth a bit as the popcorn warms to heat it evenly. As the popcorn heats, it will pop and fill the sifter. Wear asbestos gloves to prevent a burn.

INDIAN POPCORN

5 tablespoons butter or margarine, melted
1 teaspoon dried dillweed
1 teaspoon lemon pepper (or use freshly ground pepper and grated lemon zest to taste)
1 teaspoon Worcestershire sauce
1/2 teaspoon garlic powder
1/2 teaspoon onion powder
1/4 teaspoon salt
2 quarts popped corn

Mix butter, dillweed, lemon pepper, Worcestershire sauce, garlic powder, onion powder, and salt. Toss with hot freshly popped corn.

Note One-fourth cup unpopped corn makes about 2 quarts popped corn.

The state rangers stationed at the beautiful old Mission San Juan Bautista in California bake an authentic Pueblo Indian bread in an historic *hornito* on the grounds behind the Castro-Breen Adobe. The bread baking is one of the state park's scheduled activities and samples are given to the visitors who happen along at the right time.

State Park Ranger Gwen Fissel tells me: "We start the fire in the morning. Then about one to two o'clock someone pulls the fire out, brushes the ashes, and closes the door. We test for temperature by the warmth from the outside and by throwing a small amount of meal on the bottom of the oven. If the meal turns golden brown in a few seconds but does not burn immediately, the oven is ready. The bread is put in and after it's baked, we cut it up for samples."

The famous, crusty bread of the Pueblos is still baked in beehive-shaped ovens, usually as smooth round loaves, decorated beautifully with squash blossoms and other symbolic designs for special occasions.

THE RANGERS' PUEBLO BREAD AT SAN JUAN BAUTISTA

2 tablespoons active dry yeast
1/2 cup lukewarm water (110° to 115°F)
1/4 cup corn oil or other cooking oil
3 eggs
2 teaspoons salt
10 cups unbleached flour
2 cups water

Soften yeast in lukewarm water. Mix together oil, eggs, salt, and yeast mixture in a large bowl. Alternately add flour and water, a little at a time, beating thoroughly after each addition. Knead in the last of the flour until dough is very smooth. Shape into a ball and place in a large greased bowl. Cover with a dampened towel and let rise in a warm place until double in bulk. Punch down and knead on a floured board for at least 5 minutes. Divide dough into 4 sections and shape each section into a slightly flattened ball. Place balls on aluminum foil, cover with dampened cloth, and let rise for 20 to 30 minutes in a warm place. Set in a smoke oven and bake for about 40 minutes, or until tops are browned and loaves make a hollow sound when tapped.
Makes 4 loaves

The grandest and most spirited ladies on the California cooking scene are two dear old friends, Gen Callahan and Lou Richardson, who always come up with innovative ideas. When I told them I was working on ways with charcoal, they suggested I save all my egg cartons to store and stack the little briquettes. When time comes to lay the fire, I squirt on some fire lighter and strike up the match.

BLACKBERRY COBBLER, GEN AND LOU

Save your 1-pound coffee cans for the wild berry season. Rinse them well, dump about 2 cups of berries in each can, sprinkle each with 1/2 cup sugar and dot with butter, a generous dab of it. Set cans on grill and when the berries boil, drop in big spoonfuls of soft shortcake dough (Gen and Lou use biscuit mix with light cream) right on top of the berries. Cover tightly with foil, punch with a skewer so a little steam can escape, and simmer 18 to 20 minutes. Serve with light cream or ice cream.

TIN CAN BAKED APPLES

Allow 1 can for each big apple and butter it well. Beginning at the stem end of the apples, take out the cores almost to the blossom end, and fill cavities with sugar and 2 or 3 tablespoons rum. Cover tightly with foil; punch holes to allow steam to escape and set cans on grill to bake for 30 to 45 minutes.

These recipes are dedicated to an old, young friend, of wild and woolly Rancho Santa Fe.

PADDY TWOHY'S TADPOLES

Make 4 slits around the outer top side of a marshmallow. Poke in 4 milk-chocolate chips. Do the same with another marshmallow, then sandwich the two together, with the chocolate chip ends touching. Slide them onto a sharp stick and toast slowly over the coals. Guaranteed to melt in your mouth.

If you have a little ice cream handy, this will taste like apple pie à la mode.

ROASTED CINNAMON APPLES ON A STICK

Place 1 apple on the sharp end of a stick. Hold the apple near the flames or hot coals to scorch the peel until it bubbles. Remove from the fire and peel the skin off. Roll the apple in a mixture of sugar and cinnamon. Rotate the apple slowly over the coals until the melting sugar forms a glaze. Slice off the outer portion and eat it. Repeat dipping the apple into the sugar and cinnamon, toasting it and eating it until the apple is gone.

I can't think of a single time I've cooked over the coals without trying something wild and wonderful with fresh fruit. That's due to my early basic training with my dear old buddy, Galen Geller, who manages the California Tree Fruit Agreement and agreeably concurs that nothing, but nothing, is a greater complement to smoky meat and game than a peach, a pear, a nectarine, or a plum.

CHARCOAL-GRILLED FRUIT

Mixed Grill Cut fruit of choice in half, remove core and seeds or pits, and arrange in a hinged grill. Squeeze a lemon over the surfaces; sprinkle with sugar and a dash of ground cinnamon and grill quickly until just hot. Brush with melted butter. Splash a little brandy or sweet liqueur over all.

Chinese Pears Halve and core Bartlett pears, squeeze lemon juice over surfaces and brush with butter. Grill, basting with a mixture of soy sauce and honey.

Spiced Plums Make little foil packets to hold 2 or 3 plums. Dot with butter and sprinkle with brown sugar and ground allspice. Wrap tightly and toss into coals.

Sherried Peaches Halve, peel, and pit peaches, brush with butter and sprinkle with brown sugar. Set on grill to brown, turn and fill cavities with a few raisins and a spoonful of sherry.

Turkish Delights Cut a variety of fruits in chunks for skewers, alternating colors and textures. Squeeze lemon juice over all and set on grill, basting with butter. Serve with honey-flavored whipped cream and chopped pistachios.

LATIN AMERICA & THE CARIBBEAN

On all the coasts of Mexico, you are treated to great fish cooked over little fires on the beaches and in makeshift huts. You eat with your fingers, plunging the charred fish into a sauce or two, and when you have devoured more than you ever dreamed you could, you mop up in the ocean. The bright coral snapper of Mexico is lovely with the sauce of Veracruz in the Yucatán.

HUACHINANGO A LA VERACRUZANA
The Red Snapper of Veracruz

3- to 4-pound whole dressed red snapper, with
   head and tail left on
Coarse salt
Fresh lime juice

Sauce
6 medium tomatoes
3 small onions
3 cloves garlic
1/4 cup olive oil

2 bay leaves
1 cup pitted green olives
1/4 cup capers
2 fresh or pickled jalapeño chili peppers, cut
   into strips
Salt and freshly ground pepper to taste

Prick the fish on both sides with a fork. Rub in the salt and lime juice and let stand for 2 hours or so at room temperature.

Thread the tomatoes and onions on separate skewers and set on the grill; char evenly. Chop them coarsely, draining off most of the seeds and juice, and combine with the garlic and oil in a saucepan. Set on the grill and heat to boiling. Add rest of ingredients and adjust seasonings.

Lay the snapper in a hinged grill and place over the coals. Baste with a little of the sauce. Cook about 15 minutes on each side, turning once and basting with more sauce. Serve sauce on side.
Makes 6 servings

Antojito means "little whim" in Spanish. Mexicans are full of little whims; they are the most persistent noshers in the world and food vendors have astonishing cooking contraptions that they push for miles to post themselves wherever the crowds might gather in need of a bit of sustenance—floppy warm tortillas crammed with *carnitas,* bits of pork and a tingling hot sauce. I discovered long ago the best way to eat a taco is on an angle, both you and the taco, holding the far end closed and a bit raised. Bite with your teeth only, keeping your lips from any extra squeezing effect. Practice, *amigo.*

MEXICAN DEVILLED BEEF BONES

3 pounds beef ribs, in 1 piece
1 large onion, chopped
1 can (4 ounces) pimientos, chopped
2 fresh serrano chili peppers, chopped
1 clove garlic, crushed
1 teaspoon salt
1/4 teaspoon freshly ground pepper
3 tablespoons olive oil
Warm tortillas

Make deep slashes behind rib bones. Mix onion, pimientos, chilies, garlic, salt, and pepper. Press mixture into slashes. Rub meat with oil. Grill, basting with oil as necessary, until nicely browned but still pink. Cut ribs for eating out of hand in warm tortillas.
Makes 6 servings

SMOKY NACHOS ON THE GRILL

6 cups corn tortilla quarters, fried until crisp
2 cups each shredded Monterey Jack and mild cheddar cheese
1/2 cup Rajas, page 45, or
1 can (4 ounces) whole green chili peppers, cut into slivers

Poke a few holes in a double thickness of foil. Spread corn chips one layer deep, overlapping. Sprinkle with cheese, then chilies. Set on grill and heat until cheese melts. To be eaten out of hand. Makes approximately 8 servings

Here is a spicy hot Chilean *antojito.*

LOMITOS DE CHANCHO
Little Loins of Pork Grilled for Sandwiches

2-pound pork loin, sliced into 1-inch-thick steaks
1/2 cup white vinegar
1 to 2 teaspoons crushed hot red pepper
1 onion, chopped
2 cloves garlic, crushed
Salt, cayenne pepper, and freshly ground black pepper
Lard
Crusty round rolls, split

Marinate pork in a mixture of the vinegar, red pepper, onion, garlic, and seasonings for 1 hour at room temperature. Pat dry. Rub with a little lard and grill over coals. Serve in little round rolls.
Makes 8 servings

Anticuchos are the Peruvian equivalents of the Mexican "little whims." The flavor and texture of the charcoal-grilled heart of South America is absolutely superb—and surprising. When you grill it rare, it's as tender and juicy as a good steak. Indonesian *sates* and *anticuchos* are skewered with the pieces of meat about an inch apart, unlike the kabobs of most countries.

ANTICHUCHOS MIXTOS
Heart and Liver Kabobs of Peru

1 beef heart, about 2 pounds
1 pound beef liver
2 teaspoons crushed hot red pepper
3 tablespoons corn oil
1 cup red wine
1 large onion, quartered
2 cloves garlic, crushed
Juice of 1 lemon
Salt and freshly ground pepper to taste

Cut heart into 1-inch cubes, removing membrane and fat. Cut liver into same-size cubes. Marinate 2 hours or more at room temperature in rest of ingredients. Thread meats on skewers, alternating heart and liver, and leaving about 1 inch between pieces. Grill quickly over coals, brushing with marinade, until browned on the outside but still pink on the inside, about 5 minutes.
Makes 8 servings

Most Andean dishes contain *ají,* which is botanically related to the Mexican chili peppers, but with a different flavor. You don't need to taste with caution as in Mexico, but the word *arequipeño* is a hint that the first mouthful might be a kiss of fire. The mountain people of Peru have a favorite pepper that is flaming red and flaming hot, which is sliced and served in careful isolation.

ROASTED CHILIES WITH
A CHARCOAL FLAVOR

First, put on your rubber gloves. Arrange the chilies in a hinged grill and char them over the coals until the skins blister and they are evenly browned. Put them into a damp cloth or plastic bag immediately and let them sweat for about 20 minutes; the skin will peel off easily. Slit each chili down one side, leaving top ridge intact. Carefully cut out the core from under the base of the stem and remove seeds and veins. If the chilies are too strong, let them soak in a vinegar/water/salt solution for half an hour or so.

RAJAS

Simply roast chilies and peel them, as described in preceding recipe, and then cut them into strips. Use with roasted meats, fish, and chicken.

Note While you are at it, roast a head of garlic to toss in soups and stews.

In Mendoza, where the gigantic grapes are better for eating fresh than for making wine, many Argentine cooks prefer the freshly squeezed juice for their marinades and sauces. It gives an exquisitely fresh flavor to delicate game, fish, and fowl.

POLLO AL JUGO DE UVA
Chicken in Grape Juice

2 pounds muscatel or other highly flavored grapes
3-1/2-pound fryer chicken, cut into serving pieces
1/4 cup chopped fresh coriander

Squeeze the grapes with your hands until all the juice is released. Put through a sieve to remove seeds and skins. Marinate chicken in fresh grape juice and coriander for 2 hours or more. Grill over coals, turning once and brushing occasionally with juice, until nicely browned, about 30 minutes.
Makes 4 servings

Even today when transportation has broken the isolation of the *patrias chicas*—the "little home-lands"—of Mexico, you can find your way blindfolded by the smell of the food alone.

POLLO PICADO CON TOCINO
Mexican Chicken Larded with Spicy Bacon

4 thick slices bacon
2 cloves garlic
2 fresh serrano chili peppers
Pinch each ground cloves and cinnamon
3-1/2-pound roasting chicken

Lay bacon slices flat. Crush garlic with chilies and spices and spread mixture over bacon with your fingers. Cut bacon into shoestring strips and poke strips under skin of chicken, mostly over breast. Don't fuss too much as the bacon literally melts over the bird. Balance chicken on a spit or set in a smoke oven and cook until nicely browned, 1 to 1-1/2 hours.
Makes 4 servings

In his history of the conquest of Mexico, Bernal Diaz writes that Montezuma was "served with a great variety of dishes, all cooked in the native style, and they were put over small earthenware braziers to keep warm." Diaz again talks of more than thirty dishes, and over 300 plates of food, including fowls, turkeys, pheasants, local partridges, quail, wild duck, venison, wild boar, marsh birds, pigeons, and hares.

Like other gastronomic nationalists, Mexicans are very proud of their great cuisine. With good reason they resent the "continental cuisine" and *chile con carnavales* that have made inroads. This duck with its silken green sauce of pumpkin seeds is a true classic of Mexico. At the time of the Spanish conquest, Montezuma and other Aztec rulers were eating stews with tomatoes and pumpkin seeds long before the Mayans cultivated pumpkins.

PATO EN MOLE VERDE DE PEPITA
Duck with Green Pumpkin Seed Sauce

5- to 6-pound duck, cut into serving pieces
3/4 cup unsalted hulled pumpkin seeds, toasted
6 peppercorns
Pinch of cumin seeds
1 cup green tomatoes (tomatillos), husks
    removed (if using canned, drain)
4 fresh serrano chili peppers
1 medium onion
2 garlic cloves
3 sprigs each epazote* and coriander
A handful of greens (radish tops, lettuce,
    etc.—just as long as they are green)

Prick the skin of the duck with fork tines held upward to render out the fat without piercing the flesh. Grill duck 9 to 10 minutes to a side.

While duck is cooking, make the sauce. Grind the pumpkin seeds, peppercorns, and cumin seeds in a blender; set aside. Purée the rest of the ingredients and pour into a saucepan. Bring to a boil and stir in pumpkin seed mixture. Taste for seasoning and remove from fire or sauce will curdle. Serve duck with sauce—which should be very *picante*—and hot tortillas.
Makes 3 or 4 servings

*Strongly flavored herb; sometimes called Jerusalem oak pazote.

GANSO A LA POBRE
Mexican Poor Man's Goose

6 pork chops, about 1-1/2 inches thick
4 slices cold boiled ham, chopped
2 onions, chopped
Crumbled dried sage
Salt and freshly ground pepper
6 pitted prunes
Lard
A long branch of bay leaves

Have your butcher cut pockets in the chops. Combine ham and onions with sage and salt and pepper to taste. Stuff each chop with a prune and some of the ham-onion mixture. Rub chops with lard. Toss bay leaf branch onto coals and grill chops until nicely browned but not dry, about 30 minutes.
Makes 6 servings

LECHÓN ASADO CON SALSA DE NARANJA
Mexican Roast Suckling Pig
with Bitter Orange Sauce

12- to 20-pound dressed suckling pig
Coarse salt
Heart, liver, and lights of the pig, chopped
4 tablespoons butter
1 large onion, chopped
1 large tomato, peeled and chopped
4 cups stale bread cubes, soaked in milk and
   squeezed dry
1 cup raisins, soaked in
1/2 cup dry sherry
1 cup whole roasted almonds
1 tablespoon capers
Salt, freshly ground pepper, crushed hot red
   pepper, and crumbled dried sage and marjoram
Lard
Salsa de Naranja, following

Wash pig and pat dry. Rub inside and out with
coarse salt. Sauté innards in butter with onion and
tomato. Lightly mix with rest of ingredients, except lard and Bitter Orange Sauce, seasoning to
taste. Stuff the pig with mixture, truss legs in place
and secure cavity. Rub pig with lard. Balance pig
on a spit or set in a smoke oven, and place drip pan
underneath. As pig cooks, baste it with the drippings.

Meanwhile, prepare the Salsa de Naranja. Baste
pig with sauce during the last hour of roasting.
Meat thermometer should register 180° to 185°F
when pig is done. Spoon rest of sauce over carved
pork.
Makes 8 to 12 servings

Lovely with duck and lamb as well as pig.

SALSA DE NARANJA
Bitter Orange Sauce

1 cup white vinegar
1 cup sugar
6 Seville (bitter) oranges (available in late winter
   in Latin American markets)
Juice of 2 lemons
4 tablespoons butter

In a saucepan boil vinegar and sugar until it is a
pale golden syrup. Peel the zest from 3 of the
oranges and cut into thin strips. Simmer in the
syrup 10 minutes. Stir in juice of the 6 oranges,
lemon juice, and butter.
Makes approximately 3 cups

The very act of unwrapping a steaming corn husk adds to the excitement of the tamale treasure hunt. A tamale is a little pack of *masa* streaked with chili, filled with spicy meat or chicken, sometimes sweetmeats; one I had was filled with pumpkin. The market in Toluca is famous for a tamale that enfolds hundreds of inch-long fish and is baked in the ashes or on hot stones until the husks are charred. When you're in Morelia at the right time and the right place, you'll have your roasted pork —pretty as a picture, rich, dark pork with a bright red sauce and a lattice of cheese and green chilies— *con uchepos*—the fresh, green corn tamales of the region.

THE COUNTRY SPARERIBS OF MORELIA

4-1/2 pounds country-style pork spareribs
12 corn tamales wrapped in corn husks (optional)

Sauce
6 tomatoes
6 fresh serrano chili peppers
2 cloves garlic, crushed
1 teaspoon salt
White vinegar

Garnishes
1 pint sour cream
1 pound *queso blanco* (white cheese),
   cut into strips
Rajas de chiles poblanos, page 45

Grill the ribs slowly over coals until nicely browned and crisp. Meanwhile, char the tomatoes and chilies on separate skewers on the grill. Purée them in a blender, char and all. Add garlic, salt, and a splash of vinegar. Taste for seasoning. Pour into a saucepan on the edge of the grill to thicken the sauce. Toss the corn-husked tamales on the coals to heat up. Cut up the crisp ribs and serve with the tamales, the sauce, and garnishes of sour cream, cheese, and chilies.
Makes 6 servings

Brazil is a fascinating mixture of West African, primitive Indian, and Portuguese influences. The first thing you notice about Brazilian food is that many dishes are colored bright orange-yellow from the African dendê oil. The half-wild cattle have been crossed with the East Indian zebu strains for generations. The *churrasco,* a little tough and a little wild, is one of the most popular of the Brazilian meats. In the backwoods it is usually roasted with its hide on.

CHURRASCO A MODA DE SERTAO
Beef Ribs and Breast of the Backwoods

6 pounds beef ribs and breast, in 1 piece
Coarse salt
Cracked peppercorns
6 cloves garlic, crushed

Pepper and Lemon Sauce
6 pickled hot chili peppers, drained and chopped
1 large onion, finely chopped
1 clove garlic, crushed
1/2 cup fresh lemon juice
Dash of salt

Mix together all ingredients for the sauce and let stand to allow flavors to blend. Rub beef with salt, pepper, and garlic. Balance meat on a spit and cook over coals until charred and crisp on the outside and still rare on the inside. Serve with Pepper and Lemon Sauce on the side.
Makes 6 to 8 servings

If you even come upon the word "chevron" on a menu, you now know that it's simply a fancy word for goat. In all Latin American countries, the kid is highly prized right down to the tripe. Along the Tex-Mex border, where there is little prejudice, you need not be alarmed at the signs for roast kid sandwiches.

CABRITO ASADO
Mexican Roast Kid

1 leg kid with chops
4 cloves garlic, slivered
Bacon, cut into short barbs
Salt and freshly ground pepper
4 tablespoons butter
1 onion, finely chopped
1 bay leaf
1/4 cup raisins
1/2 cup Madeira

Slash meat in several places with a sharp knife. Poke a sliver of garlic and a barb of bacon into each slash. Sprinkle with salt and pepper. Melt butter in a small saucepan placed on the grill and sauté onion. Add rest of ingredients and use as a basting sauce. Balance meat on a spit or set in a smoke oven and cook, basting occasionally, until nicely browned, about 1-1/2 hours.
Makes 6 to 8 servings

The Mayan community center was the ancient cooking hole called the *pib,* fueled by charcoal that heated the big flat stones on which everything under the sun was cooked. In the Yucatán, *pibil* means food that is cooked this way, usually marinated with the achiote spice that turns everything a bright crimson. The meat is generally wrapped in plantain or banana leaves and marinated overnight before being put into the *pib.*

COCHINITA PIBIL
Pork Roast, Yucatán Style

4-1/2-pound pork loin
1 tablespoon achiote seeds, soaked in water
   to soften
4 cloves garlic
1 tablespoon peppercorns
2 whole allspice
1 tablespoon salt
2 fresh hot green chili peppers
1/4 cup Seville orange juice or white vinegar
A good pinch each cumin and coriander seeds
Banana leaves
Warm tortillas

Salsa de Naranja
1 large onion
3 fresh hot green chili peppers
1 large tomato
1 teaspoon salt
2/3 cup Seville orange juice or white vinegar

Make little slashes all over the pork. Blend rest of ingredients, except banana leaves and tortillas, to make a paste and rub it over the meat and into the slashes. Lightly sear banana leaves to make them flexible. Wrap up the meat (or use parchment paper or foil) and let marinate several hours or overnight. Set the meat in a prepared pit oven or a smoke oven and cook 3 to 4 hours, or until meat is tender enough to be shredded from the bones. While meat is cooking, blend ingredients for the Salsa de Naranja until smooth. Shred meat and pour juices accumulated in wrapping over the meat. Serve pork with plenty of warm tortillas and the salsa.
Makes 8 servings

Still locked in the gnarled clutches of the humid jungles of Central America, vestiges of the Olmec civilization, seen only by the tree-dwelling birds, an occasional foraging jaguar, and the all-too inquisitive and rather delicious iguana.

Around suppertime, smoke drifts from every doorway in Mexico, and you can smell the pungent *ocote*—thin strips of resinous pine used to fire the charcoal. If you're lucky, you might be asked in for a little grilled steak wrapped around a charred sweet chili nestled in a tortilla.

CARNE ASADA CON CHILE POBLANO
Charcoal-grilled Steak with Poblano Chilies

Skirt steaks, 1 per person
Salt and freshly ground pepper
Fresh lime juice
Fresh poblano chili peppers or canned green
    chili peppers
Warm corn tortillas
Guacamole, page 60

Trim fat from steaks with a sharp knife, slit the steaks open horizontally, and pound lightly with the side of a cleaver. Season with salt and pepper and a little lime juice. Grill fast over coals. At the same time, grill the chili peppers until nicely charred. Wrap a steak and a chili in a warm tortilla with a spoonful of Guacamole.

In Mexico City, the original Club Tampico established in the thirties gained fame with their tender little charcoal-grilled "minute" steaks. Now you can find these steaks all over Mexico, and a variation of *a la Tampiqueña* that I like even better than the traditional one is one made with *very thin* pork chops. Serve your "minute" steaks with *enchiladas de queso* topped with red and green tomato sauce, *frijoles refritos, guacamole* (page 60), *rajas de chiles poblanos* (page 45), and warm corn tortillas.

CARNE ASADA A LA TAMPIQUEÑA
Charcoal-grilled Steak in the Style of Tampico

6 tender steaks, 1/2 inch thick
Salt and freshly ground pepper
Fresh lime juice

In Tampico, the steaks are from the fillet, but you can get away with perfectly delicious skirt steaks at half the price. Simply trim the fat and flatten with the flat side of a cleaver. Season steaks with salt and pepper and a squeeze of lime. Brush ashes from your bed of coals and toss steaks directly on the coals, turning almost immediately. Have all the other goodies ready to go. *Pronto.*
Makes 6 servings

Mexicans may be shy on stoves, but you can hear the musical whirring of electric blenders everywhere. I especially love the bright, sharp flavor of sauces made with vegetables that have been charred over the coals and then tossed in the blender, stems and all. In Sonora, you can get a steak served on a flattened, charcoal-roasted potato, with a sauce *ranchero.*

BISTECES RANCHEROS DE SONORA
Country Steaks and Potatoes

6 shoulder or chuck steaks, about 1/2 inch thick
2 cloves garlic, crushed in 2 to 3 tablespoons
   olive oil
Salt and freshly ground pepper
6 baking potatoes

Sauce
3 medium onions
3 medium tomatoes
6 sprigs coriander
2 fresh serrano chili peppers
1-1/2 teaspoons salt

Rub steaks with garlic oil. Let stand. Wrap potatoes in foil and toss on the coals to cook for about 1 hour, or until tender. To make the sauce, place onions and tomatoes on separate skewers and char evenly over coals (onions will still be crisp). Coarsely chop the onions and tomatoes with the chilies and coriander in your blender or processor. Season with salt.

   Grill steaks. Slash open and flatten potatoes to make a bed for the steaks. Spoon a little sauce over all and pass the rest in a bowl.
Makes 6 servings

Elena Zelayeta cooked in the dark, for she was blind. But that didn't darken her spirits or dim her wit. Her cookbooks on Mexican food are still among the very best, her dinner parties were among the merriest, and her *barbacoa de Domingo* was a picturesque affair, indeed. I remember one lovely Sunday when she grilled skirt steaks, sliced them deftly, and served them on flour tortillas that had been rubbed with lard, seasoned with fresh oregano and baked to a pastry-like crispness. Sensational.

BARBECUED SKIRT STEAK
For a Mexican Open-faced "Pie"

2-pound skirt steak
Salt and coarsely ground pepper
2 cloves garlic, crushed
2 teaspoons crumbled dried oregano
1 tablespoon white vinegar
2 tablespoons corn oil
Flour tortillas, rubbed with lard, sprinkled with chopped fresh oregano, and baked until crisp

Rub steak with seasonings and vinegar and oil. Let stand 1 hour while you prepare tortillas. Grill steak quickly over coals, basting with marinade. Carve on the diagonal into thin slices and serve on tortillas with this good Salsa Fresca, following.
Makes 4 servings

This relish is a kissin' cousin to the popular *salsa fria* and an absolute requirement at a *barbacoa*.

SALSA FRESCA

3 large tomatoes
1 cucumber
1 green bell pepper
2 hot green chili peppers, seeded if desired
1 large onion
2 tablespoons firmly packed brown sugar
1/3 cup white vinegar
1 teaspoon salt
1/2 teaspoon each celery seeds and coarsely ground pepper

Coarsely chop all the vegetables and mix with the rest of the ingredients. Let stand several hours, covered, in your refrigerator to blend flavors.
Makes approximately 1 quart

However the local spelling runs—*bifes, biftec* or *biftek*—all are the object of a terrifying weapon with points and knobs used to whale the devil out of the notoriously tough meat of the country, except for regions in Argentina and Uruguay. All of Latin America vibrates with the vicious pounding of these little steaks. Cooks are noted for their ingenious tricks for coping with tough meat. Sometimes a rough bottom round called a *machado* (boy) is larded with so many vegetables it grows to manhood before your eyes. Here's a famous variation translated as "kill hunger."

MATAMBRE
Flank Steak Filled with Vegetables

4-pound flank steak
Salt and freshly ground pepper
Chopped fresh thyme and parsley
1 medium onion, chopped
1/4 cup red wine vinegar
1/4 cup olive oil

Filling
1 cup chopped cooked spinach
1 cup fresh green peas
1-1/2 cups bread cubes, soaked in milk and
   squeezed dry
2 tablespoons grated Parmesan or dry
   Monterey Jack cheese
Salt and freshly ground pepper
4 slender carrots
4 small hard-cooked eggs
6 slices bacon

Season the flank steak with salt, pepper, thyme, and parsley and marinate it with the onion, vinegar, and oil for 12 hours or overnight in a cool, dry place.

To prepare the filling, combine the spinach, peas, bread, and cheese. Season with salt and pepper. Lay steak out flat and spread mixture on it; place carrots and eggs evenly spaced on mixture and top with bacon slices. Roll up lengthwise and tie securely with string. Balance meat roll on a spit or set in a smoke oven and cook 1-1/2 to 2 hours, basting with marinade. Slice on diagonal to serve.
Makes 6 to 8 servings

ARROLLADO DE MATAMBRE
Argentine Meat Roll

2-pound top round steak, cut very thin
Coarse salt and pepper
2 cloves garlic, crushed
1/4 cup red wine vinegar
1 pound veal, cut into narrow strips
1/2 pound salt pork, cut into narrow strips
1/2 teaspoon crumbled dried thyme

Lay steak out flat and rub with salt, pepper, garlic, and vinegar. Let stand overnight in a cool, dry place. Arrange strips of veal and salt pork over surface. Sprinkle with thyme. Roll up lengthwise and tie securely with string. Balance meat roll on a spit or set in a smoke oven and cook, basting occasionally with marinade and turning until nicely charred, about 1-1/2 to 2 hours. Slice on the diagonal to serve.
Makes 6 servings

Probably the most picturesque traditions come from the Argentine gauchos, the nomadic, part-Indian herdsmen who roamed the pampas in the old days, living on half-wild cattle that they lassoed with an Indian weapon consisting of three balls of stone on leather thongs. Today, under the supervision of a silver-belted cook known as a *parrillero,* gaucho-sized chunks of meat are impaled on iron rods slanted to prevent the juices from dripping into the fire. There are chickens and ribs and smoked sausages, all served up with the traditional chimichurri sauce. But first, let's have a plateful of grilled cheese sprinkled with oregano.

SOUTH AMERICAN MIXED GRILL

Chimichurri Sauce, following
2 fryer chickens, quartered
Salt and freshly ground pepper
3 pounds beef chuck with ribs
Smoked beef sausages
Lemons and limes, quartered

Prepare sauce several hours ahead of time. Season chickens with salt and pepper. Trim excess fat from ribs. Slash sausages on the diagonal. Brush all meats with sauce and set chickens and ribs on grill. Cook, basting often, until nicely charred, about 45 minutes. Place sausages on grill 10 minutes before chickens and ribs are finished cooking. Serve with wedges of lemon and lime and bottles of sauce for dousing.
Makes 8 servings

CHIMICHURRI
Argentine Spiced Parsley Sauce

1/2 cup olive oil
1/4 cup red wine vinegar
1 large onion, chopped
1 clove garlic, crushed
1 small bunch parsley, finely chopped
1 small bunch coriander, finely chopped
1 teaspoon crumbled dried oregano
1/4 teaspoon cayenne pepper
1-1/2 teaspoons salt
1 teaspoon coarsely ground black pepper

Whisk together the oil and vinegar. Add rest of ingredients and let stand several hours.
Makes approximately 1-1/2 cups

GRILLED PARMESAN CHEESE

1 pound not-too-dry Parmesan cheese
Olive oil
Crushed fresh oregano leaves

With a sturdy knife, slice cheese into 1/2-inch-thick squares. Brush lightly with oil. Set in a hinged grill about 6 inches from coals and cook, turning, until cheese is slightly brown and soft but still holds its shape. Serve immediately, sprinkled with oregano —to be eaten with knife and fork and lots of *vino tinto* (red wine).
Makes 8 servings

This silken green sauce is for me the most unique, the most refreshing of all the Mexican accompaniments. I could eat a bowlful—and sometimes do—with slices of avocado and the fresh, slightly acidic cheese called *queso fresco*. Most of all, I like a good dab of both of the following sauces on charcoal-grilled anything.

SALSA DE TOMATE VERDE CRUDA
Mexican Green Tomato Sauce

4 fresh serrano chili peppers
3 green onions
2 cloves garlic
6 sprigs coriander
2 cups green tomatoes (tomatillos), husks
   removed (if using canned, drain)
2/3 cup water
Salt
Sugar

In your blender or food processor, chop all ingredients coarsely, adding water to make rather loose consistency. Season to taste.
Makes approximately 2-1/2 cups

SALSA MEXICANA CRUDA
Fresh Mexican Sauce

2 medium tomatoes
1 small onion
12 sprigs coriander
4 to 6 fresh serrano chili peppers
1 teaspoon sugar
2/3 cup fresh lime juice or orange juice or water
Salt and freshly ground pepper

Chop tomatoes, onion, coriander, and chilies coarsely and mix with sugar and juice. Season to taste.
Makes approximately 3 cups

GUACAMOLE
Avocado Sauce or "Poor Man's Butter"

1 small onion, cut up
2 fresh serrano chili peppers
4 or 5 sprigs coriander
1 large tomato, peeled
2 medium avocados
Juice of half a lemon
Salt and freshly ground pepper

In a blender, whirl onion, chili peppers, and coriander until fairly smooth. Squeeze seeds and juice from tomato (easy, when you literally do it by hand) and chop pulp coarsely. Peel avocados and mash pulp; mix with all other ingredients, seasoning with lemon juice and salt and pepper to taste.
Makes approximately 2 cups

THE CARIBBEAN

The Indians' culinary legacy to the Caribbean cuisine was to pack a fish or bird in mud, then bake it in a pit dug in the sand. When the mud was cracked away, the scales or feathers would be pulled off, leaving the flesh beautifully clean and delicate. Sometimes thyme and hot peppers or other herbs would be laid beneath the skin before roasting. The clay cookers available today serve the purpose beautifully and can be used directly in the coals or in a smoke oven.

PESCADO CON SALSA DE AGUACATE
Cuban Stuffed Fish with Avocado Sauce

1 clove garlic, minced
2 tablespoons finely chopped onion
1/4 cup dry bread crumbs
1 tablespoon minced parsley
Pinch each salt, crumbled dried thyme, crushed
    hot red pepper, and freshly grated nutmeg
1 tablespoon fresh lemon juice
1 whole dressed fish, about 3 pounds (red
    snapper, sea bass, or similar fish would be good)
3 slices lemon

Sauce
2 large ripe avocados
3 tablespoons fresh lime juice
1 tablespoon finely grated onion
1 teaspoon salt
Freshly ground pepper
3 tablespoons olive oil

Combine garlic, onion, bread crumbs, parsley, salt, thyme, red pepper, nutmeg, and lemon juice in a small bowl. Stuff cavity of fish loosely with the mixture. Secure cavity together with wooden picks. Place in clay cooking pot that has been lined with parchment paper, if unglazed. Place lemon slices over fish. Cover and place directly in the coals or in a smoke oven 45 minutes, or until fish flakes easily.

While the fish is cooking, prepare the sauce. Chop the avocados coarsely, then purée them in a food mill. Add the lime juice, grated onion, salt, and a few grindings of pepper, and mix well. Then beat in the olive oil, a teaspoon or so at a time. Taste the sauce for seasoning. The finished sauce should have the consistency of mayonnaise.

Skin the fish and place it on a platter. Spread 1 cup of the sauce evenly and thickly over the fish. Garnish the platter, as elaborately as you like, with tomatoes, parsley sprigs, olives, or sliced lime, and serve the remaining sauce on the side.
Makes 4 to 6 servings

The "higglers" or vendors on the English-speaking islands walk about the streets carrying baskets on their heads and chanting the names of their wares, mostly exotic, musical-sounding fruits. There are exotic meats as well—frog, monkey, iguana, snake, and agouti. The adventuresome always seem to agree that these all taste amazingly like veal.

CRAPAUD
"Mountain Chicken" of Dominica

1 dozen pairs frog legs
1 medium onion, finely chopped
2 cloves garlic, crushed
2 tablespoons cider vinegar
1/2 teaspoon whole cloves
Dash each salt and freshly ground pepper
Peanut oil
Lemon or lime wedges

Wash and dry frog legs. Cover with mixture of onion, garlic, vinegar, cloves, and salt and pepper. Let stand at room temperature for 1 hour, stirring occasionally. Remove from marinade. Grill over coals until brown, brushing with oil and turning frequently. Serve with wedges of lemon or lime.
Makes 6 servings

"Buy da bananas . . . catch the sweet lil' goat
Get da grouper-fish and som' cane, mon
Corn for da barbacoa and plump yams . . ."
Saturday Market, Falmouth, Jamaica, Northside

A birthday party on the Dutch island of Curaçao is an open house held from dawn until dusk and attended by everyone who remotely knows the honorée. You might be lucky enough to taste the unusual *keshy yena,* a huge Edam cheese of a casserole, hollowed out and stuffed, then baked until nicely runny and aromatic.

KESHY YENA COE CABARON
Baked Edam Stuffed with Shrimp from Curacao

1 whole Edam cheese, 3 to 4 pounds
1/2 pound small shrimp, shelled
1 medium onion, finely chopped
2 tablespoons butter
1 medium tomato, chopped
1/4 teaspoon salt
Dash each cayenne pepper and freshly ground
   black pepper
1 slice bread, crumbled
4 pimiento-stuffed green olives, sliced
1 small gherkin, chopped
1 egg, lightly beaten

Remove wax from cheese. Slice 1 inch off top and reserve. Hollow out cheese, leaving a shell 1/2 inch thick. Shred removed cheese into bits and mix with shrimp in a bowl. Set aside. Sauté onion in butter. Stir in tomato, salt, and peppers. Cook until liquid has evaporated. Add to bowl, along with remaining ingredients; toss to mix. Fill cheese cavity with mixture. Put lid in place. Wrap tightly in foil. Bake in smoke oven or in coals about 30 minutes, or until soft but still holding its shape. Serve with crusty rolls.
Makes 6 to 8 servings

Columbus noted in his journals that the natives of the islands were very strong and lived largely on a tree melon called "the fruit of the angels." This is the papaya, called the *lechosa* or *fruta bomba* on the Spanish-speaking islands (because it looks like a hand grenade) and *pawpaw* on the English-speaking islands. Its leaves and green skin have an enzyme that breaks down protein tissue and tenderizes meat. The natives wrap pork in the papaya skins, tie them on securely, and roast the meat in pits or on the coals.

"PORK DOWNTOWN" ROASTED IN PAPAYA SKINS FROM JAMAICA

5-pound pork loin
! cup firmly packed brown sugar
2 tablespoons rum
2 cloves garlic, crushed
1 teaspoon salt
1/2 teaspoon freshly ground pepper
1 tablespoon ground ginger
1/2 teaspoon ground cloves
3 bay leaves, broken
Skins of 3 papayas or 4 bananas

Score fat side of pork. Blend next 7 ingredients to make a paste, then rub into fat. Arrange bay leaves on top. Cover with papaya skins. Skewer or tie securely in place. Balance meat on spit or set in smoke oven and cook about 2 hours, or until meat thermometer registers 170°F.
Makes 6 servings

Two foods that the Europeans didn't know about before Columbus explored the Caribbean were tomatoes and hot peppers—the color and flavor of the islands. You come upon the word *Creole* everywhere you wander. Once it meant a person of pure French or pure Spanish descent, born in the New World. Now it more likely identifies a person of mixed Negro and white descent.

POULET RÔTI À LA CREOLE
Haitian Roast Chicken with Two Stuffings

1 roasting chicken, about 4 pounds
3 large bananas, chopped
1 cup cooked long-grain rice
1/4 cup pine nuts or silvered blanched almonds
2 tablespoons each fresh lime juice and rum
Salt and freshly ground pepper
1 small onion, chopped
1 clove garlic, mashed
1 tablespoon butter
1/4 cup diced cooked ham
1 cup soft bread crumbs
2 tablespoons raisins
1/2 teaspoon freshly grated nutmeg

Wash chicken and wipe dry. Make first stuffing by tossing bananas, rice, and nuts with lime juice and rum. Season to taste with salt and pepper. Fill breast cavity; truss opening. To make second stuffing, sauté onion and garlic in butter. Add ham, bread crumbs, raisins, and nutmeg. Season to taste with salt and pepper. Fill neck cavity, then skewer closed. Balance on spit or set in smoke oven and cook until thermometer registers 175°F.
Makes 4 to 6 servings

The pineapple originated in South America and migrated with the Carib Indians to the islands. During puberty rites, Carib boys were made to run through the rows of spiky pineapples to show their bravery. The fruit itself is set on doorsteps as a symbol of hospitality and is cooked on skewers along with the meat as a further gesture of graciousness.

CARIBBEAN KABOBS
Steak or Fish with Pineapple and Peppers

2 pounds top beef sirloin or firm fish fillets,
   cut into 2-inch cubes
Salt and freshly ground pepper
1/4 cup white wine vinegar
1/2 cup fresh pineapple juice
2 tablespoons molasses
1 fresh pineapple, about 4 pounds, cubed
2 medium onions, quartered
2 green bell peppers, cut into squares

Put beef cubes in bowl and season with salt and pepper. Add vinegar, pineapple juice, and molasses and toss to blend well. Let stand at room temperature for 1 hour, turning meat occasionally. Drain off marinade and reserve. Thread meat on skewers alternately with pineapple, onions, and peppers. Grill over coals until brown, turning and basting with marinade, about 5 minutes on each side.
Makes 6 servings

A bunch of bananas roasted on the coals until black and soft makes a deliciously innocent companion to meat and fish and a superb dessert with a little butter, brown sugar, and dark rum.

ANTIGUAN CHARCOAL-BAKED BANANAS

6 large ripe bananas, in 1 bunch
4 tablespoons butter
1/2 cup brown sugar
1/2 teaspoon ground allspice, or
1/2 teaspoon freshly grated nutmeg
3 limes, halved
1/4 cup dark rum, heated in a small pan placed
   on the grill

Set the bunch of unpeeled bananas in hot coals. Bake until black and soft to the touch. Meanwhile, heat butter with brown sugar and spice until bubbly. Each person should slit his banana, squeeze a lime half over it, and drizzle butter-sugar mixture on top. Ignite rum and pour it flaming over the bananas a little at a time, shaking skillet gently until the flame dies.
Makes 6 servings

The Caribbeans have a very special way with names. All the cooking in the English-speaking islands begins with a bunch of *sive*—scallions tied in the marketplace with parsley, coriander, and a branch of thyme. There are dishes called *coo-coo*, *foo-foo*, *duckunoo*. At the schooner markets, the fish have names like "go-far" (it will serve a lot of people) and "god-a-me" (it looks scared when caught).

Here is a tart and hot sauce from Haiti that is a perfect complement for grilled fish.

SAUCE TI-MALICE
Haitian Chili, Onion, and Lime Juice Sauce

1-1/2 cups finely chopped onions
1 fresh hot chili pepper, finely chopped
1 clove garlic, finely chopped
2 tablespoons peanut oil
3/4 cup fresh lime juice
Salt and freshly ground pepper

Sauté onions, chili pepper, and garlic in oil until tender but not brown. Stir in lime juice and season with salt and pepper to taste. Store in refrigerator in a jar with a tight-fitting lid.
Makes approximately 1-1/2 cups

Whatever the menu in the Spanish islands, the "cooking" almost always begins with *sofrito*, a bright mixture of tomatoes, ham, peppers, and herbs in which everything is marinated before it is cooked. You'll also get a good whiff of cinnamon and other spices, which seem to develop as the meat grills over an open fire.

SOFRITO
**The Omnipresent Tomato Marinade and
Sauce of the Spanish Caribbean**

1/4 pound each salt pork and ham, finely diced
2 onions, chopped
2 fresh hot green chili peppers, chopped
2 cloves garlic, crushed
1 pound tomatoes, peeled and chopped
A good pinch each ground cinnamon, ginger, and cloves, freshly grated nutmeg, and salt
1 teaspoon achiote seeds, soaked in water to soften and crushed (optional)
1/4 cup chopped fresh coriander or parsley

Cook pork and ham until slightly crisp. Stir in onions, chilies, and garlic; then add tomatoes with their juice and the rest of the ingredients. Bring to a boil, adding water or tomato juice to make a saucy consistency. Cool and store in refrigerator to use as a marinade and as a sauce.
Makes approximately 3 cups

In 1843, an English sea captain planted a few nutmeg trees in Grenada, thus supplying a two-in-one spice kit to the island. Nutmeg and mace are different parts of the same nut—the mace is dried and powdered and the nutmeg is graded and shipped to epicurean markets. Both are lovely complements to fish and fowl.

SPICED BUTTER FOR FISH, FROGS, OR FOWL FROM GRENADA

1/2 pound butter, softened
1 tablespoon finely chopped fresh hot chili pepper
2 cloves garlic, mashed
2 tablespoons finely chopped onion
2 tablespoons chopped parsley
1 teaspoon fresh thyme leaves
1/4 teaspoon each freshly grated nutmeg and
    ground mace
Salt and freshly ground pepper

Blend softened butter with chili pepper, garlic, onion, parsley, thyme, nutmeg, and mace. Season with salt and pepper to taste.

To use butter, wash and dry fish or fowl of choice. Spread a little spiced butter on all sides (if using whole fish, score first) and grill over coals.
Makes approximately 1 cup

Oysters grow on trees in Trinidad. It sounds like the lyrics to a calypso song but, indeed, I saw them with my very eyes. The mangrove tree oyster grows along the muddy riverbanks and is delicate and delicious.

PEPPER WINE OR PEPPER RUM FROM TRINIDAD
For Dipping Oysters, Crab, or Little Grilled Fish

1 cup dry sherry or light rum
3 fresh hot chili peppers, each about 3 inches long
1 sprig thyme
1 bay leaf
3 slices lemon

Put all ingredients in a bottle with a cork or lid and let stand until flavors develop. When the wine "catches fire," use it sparingly with grilled shellfish or fish.
Makes approximately 1 cup

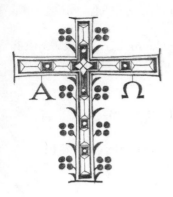

NORTHERN EUROPE

FRANCE

The great Escoffier Himself grew up in the land of the *feu de bois,* where the best food is cooked simply over charcoal and grapevine cuttings, with a handful of fresh herbs tossed over the coals. At the little, musty Escoffier museum outside Nice, you'll read about how he rose to become the master chef of all the Ritz hotels, creator of thousands of new dishes in the lofty realm of the *haute cuisine,* never forgetting the uncomplicated cooking of his early years. As you light your *feu de bois,* remember Escoffier's lifelong credo: *Faites simple*—make it simple!

This is the age-old method of grilling fish in Provence—decorative and delicious. Several slanting incisions are made on each side of scaled, cleaned fish, then the fish is rolled in olive oil. In each incision is placed a frond of fresh fennel, or little branches of rosemary or thyme. During the cooking, the fish is basted with a branch of herbs soaked in olive oil. Here's another Provençal way.

CRACKLY CRUSTED SEA BASS WITH HERBS

3-1/2-pound sea bass
Coarse salt and pepper
Olive oil
1/2 cup mixed minced fresh herbs of choice
  (parsley, tarragon, chives, thyme)
1-1/2 cups coarse dry bread crumbs

Have your fish, including head, split open, but not divided, so it will lie flat on the grill. Sprinkle inside with salt and pepper. Brush with oil and press herbs, then bread crumbs, firmly into the flesh on both sides. Dot with more oil. Grill on both sides in hinged grill, turning when crumbs are a crusty brown and fish flakes, about 15 minutes on each side.
Makes 4 servings

The *demoiselles* of Cherbourg are enough to lure anyone to the Brittany Coast. A *demoiselle* is a small lobster too fragile to export. The "girls" are grilled in their shells over very hot coals, miraculously without toughening their flesh. This is the best way to cook any kind of shellfish over the coals.

BROILED WHOLE LOBSTER

Douse your lobster in salt water. Broil it over hot coals, allowing about 15 to 20 minutes cooking time. Turn to cook evenly. Split lobster open carefully with scissors and pull out the intestinal vein and stomach. Set clarified butter on the grill to heat and lightly brown. Brush with butter and serve with a pile of lemon wedges.

OYSTERS GRATINÉED

24 oysters in the shell
4 shallots, chopped
1/4 pound unsalted butter
Salt and freshly ground pepper
Fresh lemon juice
Toasted dry bread crumbs

Put the oysters, rounded side down, on the grill for a few minutes until they pop open. Remove top shells to expose oysters. Sprinkle with shallots, dot with butter, sprinkle with salt and pepper, drizzle with lemon juice, and top with toasted crumbs. Set on grill to heat.
Makes 4 servings

I always thought *coquilles Saint-Jacques* was the creation of some chef, until I happened upon the gala opening of the scallop season in Dinard. That's the name of the scallop itself, the best in the world. Take care to grill them fast for scallops can get quite tough about it.

COQUILLES SAINT-JACQUES
AS THEY DO THEM IN BRITTANY

36 large scallops
6 limes, cut into thick slices (save ends)
1/2 pound thinly sliced bacon, each slice
    rolled up like a jelly roll
1/4 pound butter, melted
Grated Parmesan cheese

Alternate scallops with lime slices and rolls of bacon on long skewers. Squeeze ends of lime over all, brush with butter, and sprinkle with cheese. Grill quickly over coals until bacon is slightly crisp.
Makes 6 servings

The main features of Provençal cooking are garlic, fragrant herbs, and olive oil. Garlic has its own poets who have described it as the "Provençal truffle" and "the divine condiment." In this classic, the garlic literally melts into the butter sauce. And to gild the lily, extra cloves of cooked garlic are passed around for an extra squeeze over the birds.

SQUAB OR CHICKEN WITH 40 CLOVES OF GARLIC

4 small squabs, game hens, or chickens
1/4 pound butter
40 unpeeled cloves garlic
1 cup chicken stock
2 tablespoons cognac
Salt and freshly ground pepper
Bread planks

Truss birds and lightly rub with some of the butter. Balance birds on a spit or set in a smoke oven 45 minutes to 1 hour or until tender, catching drippings in a drip pan. Meanwhile, put garlic in a saucepan with rest of butter and chicken stock and simmer, covered, on the side of the grill. When garlic is tender, set aside 12 cloves and put the rest of the cloves through a sieve into the butter broth. Add the drippings and cognac, and season with salt and pepper. Serve birds on bread planks that have been toasted on the grill. Spoon sauce over, and pass reserved cloves of garlic.
Makes 4 servings

Five illustrious French chefs got together for a *magnifique pique-nique* on Long Island with wives, kids, dogs, and—*zut alors*—sand, splinters, and a crisis, no pork liver for the pâté. However, chefs Franey, Pepín, Fessaguet, Vergnes, and Verdon pulled it off in grand style. You might try out the menu: beef salad, mussels, liver pâté, cold stuffed lobsters, bluefish in white wine, green beans and tomatoes vinaigrette, marinated weakfish, vegetable salad, potato salad, mixed fresh fruit in watermelon baskets, cheeses. The *pièce de resistance,* however, were squabs amusingly flattened to resemble toads. I heartily recommend this way of grilling all kinds of birds.

PIGEONNEAUX EN CRAPAUDINE
Squabs or Chickens Flattened to Resemble Toads

4 game birds or small chickens
1/2 lemon
Salt
1/2 cup butter
1/4 cup *fines herbes* (parsley, chervil, chives, and tarragon)
Bread planks

With a sharp knife or poultry shears, cut birds open down the back. Spread out, skin side up, and press down to flatten. Run a skewer through the legs to keep flat. Rub with the lemon, salt, and butter, then press herbs into skin. Grill over coals, about 8 minutes for each side. Just before serving, set bread planks on grill to toast as a bed for the birds.
Makes 4 servings

I learned this nifty trick of covering wild birds with buttered grape leaves at a most memorable dinner for about 600 Chevaliers de Tastevin in Burgundy. I was allowed in the kitchens of the Clos de Vougeot, where I made myself small as a mouse for about a week and watched the hierarchy of chefs and sous-chefs, some thirty of them, prepare the fabulous feast. As the days passed, the temperature and temperament soared, and a regular army of servers appeared and carried the banquet off without a hitch. And I was invited to sit down and eat with the chefs. *Magnifique!*

SPIT-ROASTED GROUSE OR OTHER WILD BIRD

1 bird per person, about 1-1/2 pounds each
Small apples, cut into chunks and seasoned with
    salt and freshly ground pepper
Fatback or bacon, cut into lardoons
Buttered fresh grape leaves (or soak bottled ones
    from Greece for 1 hour to remove salt)
Salt and freshly ground pepper
Bread planks (2 for each bird)

Lard each bird with 3 or 4 strips of fatback or bacon and stuff with chunks of apple. Cover breast and legs with buttered grape leaves and tie securely. Balance birds on a spit and set bread under birds to catch the drippings. Roast until they are rich brown on the outside and rare inside, about 20 to 30 minutes. Remove apples and discard. Cut each bird in half and place cut side down on the juice-drenched bread. No sauce at all. Maybe some sautéed wild mushrooms?

ROAST DUCK WITH TURNIPS

2 Long Island ducklings, about 4-1/2 pounds each
Salt and freshly ground pepper
16 small turnips, parboiled
16 small onions, parboiled
A good pinch of duck herbs*
1/2 cup Madeira
1 cup crushed tart green grapes

Wash and dry ducklings thoroughly. Prick all over with a fork, taking care not to pierce the flesh. Season with salt and pepper. Balance ducklings on a spit. Combine duck herbs, Madeira, and grape juice to use for a basting sauce. Roast ducklings, basting with Madeira mixture, until nicely browned but still pink and juicy, about 1 hour and 15 minutes or until tender. About halfway through the roasting, skewer onions and turnips and set over coals to grill, basting frequently with the Madeira mixture.
Makes 8 servings

*A pounded mixture of dried basil, oregano, savory, fennel, and rosemary, with proportions according to taste.

This is a feast from Normandy—to each his own chicken breast with a crisp portion of duck sauced with Calvados and garnished with tart green apples with raisins, and a clump of crisp watercress or parsley.

ROAST DUCK AND CHICKEN BREASTS "BONHOMME NORMANDE"

To Roast the Duck
Wash and pat dry a 4- to 5-pound Long Island duckling. Pull out excess fat from cavity. Season cavity with salt and freshly ground pepper and stuff with a quartered lemon and onion. Remove neck and tail and truss openings. Tie legs together and twist wings under back. Rub skin with softened butter. Balance duck on a spit or set in a smoke oven (preferably over soaked apple wood chips and charcoal) and place a drip pan underneath. Roast 1 hour, then prick skin to release fat into drip pan. Brush with melted apple jelly and continue roasting and basting until duck is brown and crisp. The French prefer duck on the pink side, about 145° to 155°F on a meat thermometer.

To Roast the Chicken
This is split-second timing for beautifully moist chicken, but you can make up the foil packages early in the game and toss them on the coals while you're carving the duck. Put 8 split and boned chicken breasts between 2 layers of plastic wrap. Pound thickest part lightly with mallet. On 4 12-inch squares of foil, shape breasts into ovals (2 breasts, side by side on each). Season breasts with salt and freshly ground pepper, a squeeze of lemon juice, and a teaspoon or so of butter. Wrap to make snug flat packages, folding ends up. Toss on coals for 8 minutes exactly. You can do this during final browning period of the duck, if you prefer. Remove from foil just before serving.

To Make the Green Apples with Calvados
On the side of the grill in a skillet, heat 3/4 cup butter and stir in 1 quart of tart green apple slices. Heat 5 or 10 minutes until apples are barely tender, then stir in 1/2 cup golden raisins, a good squeeze of lemon juice, and 1/2 cup each of sugar and Calvados (apple brandy). Serve over duck and chicken.
Makes 8 servings

Cyrano de Bergerac *On the subject of Don Quixote:*
Cyrano: Am I attacking people who turn in every breeze?
De Guice: What a windmill with its long canvas-covered
arms hurls you into the mud!
Cyrano: Or rather among the stars!

The word *lèchfrite* means "lick fry" and applies to the bread planks or bread baskets arranged under the game birds to catch the drippings as the birds turn on the spit.

THE NOBLE PARTRIDGES
OF GRENOBLE WITH GRILLED PEARS

4 partridges, about 1 pound each
1 pound salt pork, cut into 24 lardoons about
    6 inches long
1/2 cup kirsch
4 buttered bread planks sprinkled with chopped
    fresh herbs of choice
8 pear halves
Melted butter

Truss birds. Wash salt pork and soak in kirsch. Lard partridges, using 2 lardoons on each side of the breast and 1 lardoon, cut in half, in gashes down each leg. (This uses 6 lardoons per bird.) Balance birds on a spit over bread planks to catch the drippings. Average cooking time is about 20 minutes. Halfway through, dip pear halves in melted butter and set on grill until nicely browned. Serve each bird on a bread plank and garnish with grilled pear halves.
Makes 4 servings

From the region of Perigord, a French goose with a favorite French delicacy of the neck skin stuffed with *pâté de foie gras*.

FRENCH GOOSE

6- to 8-pound young goose with liver
1/2 lemon
Salt and freshly ground pepper
1/2 pound dried apricots
1/2 pound pitted prunes
2 medium tart green apples
2 medium onions
2 cups roasted chestnuts, page 32, peeled
1/4 pound butter
1 cup dry bread crumbs
1 teaspoon crumbled dried sage
1/2 pound *pâté de foie gras*

Rub goose with lemon. Dry thoroughly and sprinkle inside and out with salt and pepper. Coarsely chop goose liver, fruit, onions, and chestnuts. Sauté lightly in butter. Add bread crumbs, sage, and salt and pepper to taste. Remove neck, leaving enough skin to skewer to back of bird. Stuff and truss bird. Balance bird on a spit or set in a smoke oven, placing a drip pan underneath. Prick skin with a fork and roast for 2-1/2 hours until nicely browned and tender. Meanwhile, pull neck from skin, leaving a "casing" as for sausage. Tie off one end and stuff with the pâté. Tie off other end. Brush with goose drippings and grill evenly over the coals. This lagniappe, a slice for everyone, is a succulent prelude to the feast.
Makes 6 servings

The provinces of Alsace and Lorraine have often been under German domination, and this is reflected in their food. Their grilled sausages with sauerkraut and sharp mustard are perfect together. A whole pig's foot is sometimes used to stuff a plump chicken to keep it moist and sometimes it's grilled this way.

ALSATIAN GRILLED PIGS' FEET

6 long pigs' feet
2 cloves garlic
1 large onion, stuck with cloves
1 bay leaf
2 tablespoons white vinegar
1-1/2 teaspoons salt
6 peppercorns
2 eggs, lightly beaten
Fresh bread crumbs, seasoned with herbs
    if desired

Wrap each foot in cheesecloth to keep it from breaking during the long cooking. Put the feet in a kettle with garlic, onion, bay leaf, vinegar, salt, peppercorns, and enough water to cover. Cover tightly and simmer 4 hours or until meat is tender. Cool. Dip each into egg, then into bread crumbs, coating well. Grill over charcoal until brown and crusty.
Makes 6 servings

Grilled Oxtail Discs Parboil 2 pounds of oxtail discs in the same kettle with the pigs' feet. Dip them in the eggs and crumbs and grill them until toasty over the coals for a nifty hors d'oeuvre.

Sweetbreads have a wonderful smoky flavor when cooked over the coals. Before they are grilled they must first be blanched and then, as the French say, "refreshed"–plunged in cold water.

BROCHETTES DE RIS DE VEAU
Skewered Sweetbreads

2 pairs sweetbreads
Pinch of salt
1 or 2 tablespoons white vinegar
2 large red bell peppers, cut into 1-1/2 inch squares
1/2 pound lean, thickly sliced, unsmoked bacon,
    cut into 1-1/2-inch squares, blanched 2 minutes,
    refreshed, and patted dry
Melted butter
Chopped fresh tarragon

Place sweetbreads in a saucepan with salt, vinegar, and water to cover. Bring to a boil and then simmer 3 to 5 minutes. Immediately plunge sweetbreads into cold water. When cool enough to handle, pull off the membrane, press them under a weight, and let stand for 1-1/2 hours. Then cut the sweetbreads into 1-1/2-inch pieces. Thread them onto skewers alternately with pieces of pepper and bacon. Brush with butter and cook over coals about 5 minutes, basting with more butter. Serve sprinkled with tarragon.
Makes 6 servings

My friend Mary Lyons, who is the Public Relations Director for the Food and Wines from France, remembers a certain, special dinner in Bordeaux where she was one of the guests of Monsieur and Madame Cruse in their sixteenth-century château, La Dame Blanche. There was a fireplace at one end of the dining room with a well in which you could stand up six feet tall, on either side copper cauldrons full of lilacs. A spitted lamb, redolent of fresh herbs, danced and turned during the first courses. And when it came time for dessert, the flan was dusted with sugar and annointed with cognac. A poker was laid over the coals, and when it was red hot, Monsieur le Glazier (or whatever he was called) quickly seared the top of the giant flan in crisses and crosses.

SPITTED LAMB OR KID WITH MINT AND GARLIC

4- to 7-pound leg of lamb or other cut
6 cloves garlic, coarsely crushed
Salt and freshly ground pepper
1/2 cup chopped fresh mint or parsley
Olive oil

Get a leg that's short and fat with a rosy tan color. Have your butcher remove the bone at the knee joint, leaving in the shank bone so you can use it as a handle for carving. The day before, make a mixture of the garlic, salt and pepper, and the herbs. Add a little olive oil to loosen it up a bit. Make gashes in the lamb with a sharp knife and stuff in a little of the garlic-herb mixture, inserting some in the pocket where the bone was removed. Now massage the meat all over with olive oil. Wrap it up in foil and refrigerate overnight.

Two or 3 hours before serving, remove foil and massage again with oil and let it come to room temperature. Push the spit rod through alongside the shank bone and bring it out the other end at a point where it is balanced. Place spit over the coals. *After* the meat has formed a good crust, about 20 minutes, sprinkle with salt and a good twist of pepper. Cook until meat thermometer reaches 130°F for medium rare.
Makes 6 to 8 servings

Note I like the thrifty French method of tackling a leg of lamb or kid. Hold the shank in your left hand at an angle to the carving board. Carve thick slices from the fleshy side, one slice to a person, then a slice from the shank end—called *la souris* or "the mouse." Dip rounds of French bread in the juices as you carve.

The charming art of wood carving is evident in the coats of arms of many European restaurants, particularly those of France . . . wherein the Old World wild rabbit is incorporated into their seals and more than often into their spits as cuisses de lièvre rôties.

When I was slaving over a hot stove in Paris, the freshest breath of air was along the rugged coast of Brittany where everything smelled and tasted of the sea—even the vegetables. Seaweed gathered along the ocean at low tide is used as fertilizer in the farm gardens and when nice and dry, it is tossed on the little fires along the beaches. The fabulous lamb is called *pre-salé* for the salty flavor the aromatic grasses impart to the meat. I've added some anchovies to give you just a taste of the sea with your lamb.

BUTTERFLIED LEG OF LAMB, TY-COZ
The Old Homestead in Breton Dialect

1 cup each red wine and beef stock
2 tablespoons red wine vinegar
1 tablespoon each crumbled dried rosemary and
   marjoram, and minced dried onion
1 large bay leaf, broken
5- to 6-pound leg of lamb, boned and butterflied
3 cloves garlic, slivered
6 anchovy fillets, rinsed of salt and cut up
Salt and freshly ground pepper to taste

Simmer the wine, stock, vinegar, and herbs for 10 minutes. Make small slashes in flattened-out lamb and poke in garlic slivers and anchovy fillets. Sprinkle with salt and pepper and rub wine marinade into meat. Place meat fat side up on grill over coals and cook 50 minutes to 1 hour, basting frequently and turning meat occasionally. To carve, slice across the grain.
Makes 6 servings

Doux means "gentle," *feu* means "fire." Put together you have *doufeu,* which is an ancient French cooking pot designed with an inverted lid to hold ice to promote condensation within the heavy pot when it is surrounded by hot coals. A few years ago, an iron foundry in the little village of Ancerville chose to revive the old pot and they are now available in this country. Or you can use a heavy Dutch oven and invert the lid with a layer of foil between it and the oven. The tender aromatic veal is lovely with sausages done over the coals.

VEAL STEW DOUFEU
WITH SMOKED SAUSAGES

4 pounds veal for stew
2 slices bacon, cut into small pieces
1/4 pound butter
1/2 cup water
1/2 cup minced mixed fresh herbs (parsley,
   thyme, savory, tarragon, chives)
Salt and freshly ground pepper to taste
6 French pork sausages
Chopped fresh parsley

Cut veal into bite-sized pieces. Put veal, bacon, butter, water, herbs, salt, and pepper into your *doufeu* or Dutch oven. Cover with lid filled with ice (or inverted lid of Dutch oven with a piece of foil between lid and pot). Surround with hot coals and let simmer 2 hours or until veal is tender. Grill sausages over coals until evenly browned. Add to veal and sprinkle with parsley.
Makes 6 servings

The Vicomte François Réné de Chateaubriand and the famed gourmet Brillat-Savarin were at dinner in a Parisian restaurant when the *patron* announced that he had prepared a new specialty in honor of Chateaubriand's latest novel—a succulent tenderloin encased between two slices of flank steak symbolizing Christ between two thieves. The outer steaks were seared black and discarded, leaving the tenderloin lovingly protected, juicy and rare. To this day the Chateaubriand is considered the most aristocratic of the beef cuts. I forget the "thieves" and simply marinate the steak.

CHATEAUBRIAND

2-pound diagonally cut tenderloin (cut
   from the center)
1/2 cup olive oil
Juice of 1 lemon
2 cloves garlic, crushed
Coarse salt and pepper

Have your butcher cut the steak from the center of the tenderloin. Rub it with rest of ingredients and let stand at room temperature for several hours. Grill over coals to desired doneness, 12 to 15 minutes to a side for rare. Slice on the diagonal and serve with juices and Grilled Mushroom Caps Filled with Sauce Béarnaise, following.
Makes 4 servings

GRILLED MUSHROOM CAPS
FILLED WITH SAUCE BÉARNAISE

1 tablespoon minced shallots or green onions
1 teaspoon crumbled dried tarragon
1/4 cup white wine vinegar
1/4 cup dry white wine
3 egg yolks
1/4 pound unsalted butter, melted
Salt and freshly ground pepper
12 very large mushroom caps, stems removed
Olive oil flavored with crushed cloves of garlic
Watercress

Boil shallots and tarragon with vinegar and wine in a small saucepan until liquid is reduced to about 2 tablespoons. Heat butter until bubbling. In your blender at high speed, blend egg yolks with herb mixture and gradually add butter in a slow steady stream until mixture is thick and smooth. Rub mushrooms with garlic oil. Arrange mushrooms in a hinged grill and cook over the coals along with the steak. Pour warm béarnaise into mushroom caps and over steaks. Garnish with watercress.
Makes 6 servings

One of the easiest and best steaks is fixed with coarse crushed peppercorns, *au poivre* in French. This method is used in almost every province and is good with fish and duck as well.

STEAK AU POIVRE PROVENÇALE

2 tablespoons black tellicherry peppercorns
4 thick club or New York steaks, rubbed with
    garlic cloves and olive oil
2 large ripe tomatoes, cut into 4 thick slices
Salt and freshly ground pepper
1/4 cup cognac or brandy, warmed in a small
    pan placed on the grill
Softened butter mixed with minced fresh herbs
    of choice

Crush peppercorns with a mortar and pestle. With the heel of your hand, pound some of the pepper onto both sides of each steak. Let stand while you prepare the coals. Grill steaks over coals to desired doneness, placing tomato slices on grill when you turn the steaks. Top each steak with a slice of grilled tomato and sprinkle with salt and pepper. Flame with cognac and top with a dollop of herb butter.
Makes 4 servings

FISH AU POIVRE

4 firm fish steaks, about 1 inch thick (swordfish
    and salmon are good choices)
Salt
2 tablespoons peppercorns
1/4 cup cognac or brandy, warmed in a small pan
    placed on the grill
Softened butter mixed with minced fresh herbs
    of choice

Season fish with salt. Crush peppercorns with a mortar and pestle. With heel of your hand, press pepper into both sides of steaks. Grill 5 minutes to a side. Flame with cognac and top with a dollop of herb butter.
Makes 4 servings

DUCK AU POIVRE

3-1/2-pound duckling
1/2 lemon
Salt
1 tablespoon peppercorns
1/4 cup cognac or brandy, warmed in a small pan
    placed on the grill

Wash duckling and dry well. Rub with lemon and salt. Dry thoroughly. Prick with fork, taking care not to pierce flesh. Crush peppercorns with a mortar and pestle. Press breast of duck firmly into pepper, then press remaining pepper into legs. Balance duck on a spit and roast until nicely browned, about 50 minutes to 1 hour. Flame with cognac before serving.
Makes 3 or 4 servings

FILLET WITH ROQUEFORT CHEESE

1 large clove garlic, crushed
1/2 pound Roquefort cheese
4 tablespoons butter, softened
2 teaspoons dry mustard
Dash of Worcestershire sauce
4 *filets mignons*

Mix together garlic, cheese, butter, mustard, and Worcestershire sauce until smooth. Grill steaks on one side, turn, and spread with cheese mixture. Continue grilling to desired doneness.
Makes 4 servings

A few years ago, I ate my way through the annual gastronomic fair in Dijon, the principal city of Burgundy. The big mellow Burgundy wines scented the very air, to say nothing of the many regional dishes that you could sit down and eat in the transported regional restaurants. And I had, among a thousand other things:

FONDUE BOURGUIGNON, FEU DE BOIS

A nice idea for a do-it-your-way steak party. Cut top sirloin or other good quality steak into bite-sized chunks. Then prepare a good selection of dipping sauces in advance. (Among the condiments that come in bottles and jars you might include a selection of good mustards, chutney, horseradish sauce.) Supply long forks or green sticks for everyone and let them skewer and char their own steak.

SPITTED BEEF IN A PROVENÇAL BLANKET

3-pound short loin or sirloin of beef
1-1/2 pounds thickly sliced bacon
4 ounces anchovy fillets
A little beef marrow
2 medium onions
3 cloves garlic
1 large tomato, peeled and squeezed of juice
Fresh basil, savory, thyme, and parsley
   (a small bunch)

Tell your butcher you want a first-rate piece of beef, the right shape and size for your spit (or smoke oven). Now lay out 1 pound of the bacon vertically, each slice overlapping so as to make a flat "blanket" large enough to go around the beef. Chop the rest of the bacon and other ingredients coarsely. Spread over bacon. Set beef horizontally in center and carefully wrap bacon blanket around it. Tie securely with string and cover with foil, including ends. Balance meat on a spit or set in a smoke oven and roast 20 to 30 minutes per pound, depending on how rare you want it (1 to 1-1/2 hours). Carefully remove foil and continue roasting until crust is a beautiful mahogany brown.
Makes 6 servings

Note For the final browning, hickory chips and herbs may be added to the coals. This is also lovely served cold.

ANTELOPE, REINDEER, VENISON
WITH JUNIPER SAUCE
Or, What Has Your Hunter Bagged?

1/2 pound salt pork
1/2 cup brandy
2 carrots
2 medium onions
2 teaspoons salt
4 bay leaves
A few sprigs each rosemary, thyme, and parsley
1/2 cup each red wine vinegar and olive oil
2 fifths good claret
4 to 5 pounds game of choice

Poach salt pork a few minutes in boiling water to remove some of the salt; drain and cut into strips for larding. Soak strips in brandy while you make the marinade.

Choose a pot that will hold your game fairly snug. Chop vegetables coarsely. Toss in the pot with the salt, herbs, oil, vinegar, and 1 fifth of the wine. Using salt pork strips (reserve brandy), lard the game with the grain of the meat straight through to the center. Add reserved brandy to marinade. Lower game into pot and add remaining wine to cover. Cover pot and let marinate, refrigerated, 2 or 3 days, turning meat occasionally.

Remove game from marinade and reserve marinade for sauce. Pat the meat dry with paper towels. Balance meat on a spit or set in a smoke oven, placing drip pan underneath to collect juices for the sauce. Roast until meat is cooked, 135°F on a meat thermometer for rare. Game meats are always best when rare—and they can get quite tough about it. Let stand while you make the Juniper Sauce, following.
Makes 10 to 12 servings

JUNIPER SAUCE

6 each juniper berries and bottled green
    peppercorns, drained
Drippings from roasting meat
1 cup or more reserved game marinade, strained
2 tablespoons brandy
Salt and freshly ground pepper
Sugar

Crush the juniper berries and peppercorns with a mortar and pestle. Add to game drippings, along with the marinade. Boil hard to reduce. Add the brandy and season with salt, pepper, and sugar until you get a perfect sweet-sour sauce.
Makes approximately 1 cup

Charlemagne's rule was called the "silent centuries" with regard to the design of an epicurean meal. But Merlyn, having traveled the heights and caverns of history, both past, present, and even future, desired a repast of ribaldly visual and tactile delight. In the roaring fire and on beds of vermillion charcoal, joints of lean beef and mutton, delicate breasts of spring partridge, smoked eel from that floating kingdom of Buddha and from a region not yet "discovered," ground pebbles of sirloin fired to a leathery texture and drowned with a purée of love-apple.

BELGIUM

When Belgium-born Jeanne Sanders and I were working toward our *diplôme* at La Varenne, the cooking school in Paris, we usually dragged ourselves home on the Metro smelling like fishmongers. One of our teacher-chefs, Chambret, had a formidable reputation—and an incredible repertoire of ingenuous ways with fish. We gutted, scaled, boned, *tous les jours*. And now that Jeanne has a formidable reputation as a teacher-chef at the Alliance Française in Houston, she shares this lovely almond-scented trout with us.

TRUITE EN PÂTÉ D'AMANDES
Trout in Almond Paste

4 tablespoons butter
Juice of 2 lemons
Grated lemon zest
Salt and freshly ground pepper
4 river trout
1/4 cup finely ground roasted almonds
1 tablespoon chopped fresh thyme, or
1 teaspoon crumbled dried thyme

Cream butter and mix it with lemon juice, and lemon zest, salt, and pepper to taste. Brush trout with butter and roll them in ground almonds, pressing slightly with fingertips to make sure almonds adhere. Sprinkle with thyme and place in hinged grill. Cook over coals, 2 to 3 minutes a side.
Makes 4 servings

Brussels! Here a *patisserie*, there a *confiserie*, everywhere a *charcuterie*. The heart of the city is one big farmers' market with names like Rue au Buerre (Butter Street), Rue des Harengs (Herring Street) and Rue Chair et Pain (Meat and Bread Street). As you amble down Rue des Bouchers (Butcher Street), you are aware that steak and *pommes frites* is obviously the national favorite, but there is literally nothing you can't get in this rich and varied cuisine.

PORK LOIN WITH
A HEART OF GREEN PEPPER BUTTER

5- to 6-pound pork loin
1 tablespoon bottled green peppercorns, drained
1 small clove garlic
1/2 teaspoon ground cinnamon
2 tablespoons chopped fresh coriander or parsley
4 tablespoons butter
Salt and freshly ground pepper
Madeira
Orange slices

Have your butcher bone the loin and slash it about halfway through lengthwise. Save the bones in one piece for a rack. Crush the green peppercorns with the garlic and cinnamon. Mix with coriander and butter and season with salt and pepper. Spread pepper butter down into pocket of pork. Tie securely. Set pork on the rack of bones in a smoke oven or balance loin on a spit. Roast, basting with Madeira, 1-1/2 hours or until a meat thermometer registers 160°F. Garnish with orange slices.
Makes 6 servings

BRITISH ISLES

Even if their cooking isn't always so hotsy-totsy, one of the marvelous things about the British is that they behave precisely as you might hope—witty, wry, polite, proud, ever hospitable—as if to agree with Hilaire Belloc that being born British is akin to winning first prize in the lottery of life. To accommodate me in my pursuit of some British fire and smoke, a good old friend in Dorset put together a weird "barbecue" over which he grilled this magnificent hare.

MACDONALD'S JUNIPER BERRY HARE
A Jolly Good Marinade for Most Anything

5-pound hare, cut into serving pieces
3 bay leaves, crumbled
2 cloves garlic, crushed
1 tablespoon juniper berries, crushed
1 teaspoon each crumbled dried rosemary and
    thyme (or substitute fresh)
3 onions, chopped
6 shallots, chopped
1 fifth claret
8 thick slices streaky bacon
Hickory chips for fuel

Arrange pieces of hare in a shallow dish. In a bowl mix bay leaves, garlic, juniper berries, herbs, onions, and shallots. Pat over hare. Gently pour wine over all. Cover and marinate 2 hours or so. Pat each piece dry. Grill hare over coals and hickory chips until beautifully browned. Grill bacon and serve with hare.
Makes 4 servings

My old friend, John Seymour, owns a sixty-two-acre cooperative farm in Wales where he practices his own gospel, *The Guide to Self Sufficiency* (Popular Mechanics Press), producing a lot of food off a small acreage with a high input of labor and a very low input of petrochemicals. The old farmhouses in Wales have big *simnai fawrs,* or open chimneys, and these are given a twist so that you can hang salt-cured bacon or ham out of the rain while they smoke over oak for a week.

SIMNAI FAWR SMOKED HAM AND HERBS
Welsh Chimney-smoked Ham with Herbs

4 thick smoked ham steaks, about 1 inch thick
Corn oil seasoned with bay leaf, garlic, a branch
    of thyme, and some dried hot chili peppers
4 large tomatoes
1/2 cup apple cider or white wine
1/2 cup finely chopped mixed fresh herbs (basil,
    tarragon, parsley, sorrel)
Salt and freshly ground pepper

Brush ham steaks with seasoned oil and let stand. Spear tomatoes on a long-handled fork or skewer and turn slowly over the coals until nicely charred. Cool. Squeeze out juice and seeds and discard. Heat pulp on the side of the grill in a small saucepan with the rest of the ingredients, crushing with a wooden spoon. Grill steaks until nicely browned, brushing with additional oil. Serve ham steaks with a spoonful of sauce. Potato pancakes make a good accompaniment.
Makes 4 servings

Frog legs, chicken legs, turkey legs—any legs will do. Even trotters of lamb or pork are perfectly delicious grilled slowly over the coals.

FROG LEGS FROM
THE KING'S FROG POND

12 pairs frog legs
1 cup milk
Salt, freshly ground pepper, and paprika
2 cloves garlic, crushed
Equal parts olive oil and butter
Chopped parsley
Lots of lemon wedges

Soak the frog legs in the milk for 1 hour or so. Drain. Season with salt and pepper and dust with paprika. Thread on a long skewer or individual skewers and cook over the coals, basting with a mixture of garlic, butter, and oil. When lightly brown and still juicy, serve frog legs with chopped parsley and lemon.
Makes 4 servings

The boar's head celebration became an annual event long ago at Queen's College, Oxford, when a student reading Aristotle in the forest of Shotover, was allegedly attacked by a ferocious open-mouthed wild boar. The resourceful student jammed the text down the throat of his assailant and delivered the animal to the chief steward who prepared it for Christmas dinner. Ever since, the college has commemorated the feat by partaking of a mighty boar's head each Yuletide season.

It has to be the most super supermarket in the whole wide world—the one and only Harrod's Food Hall where you're apt to meet all your fine-feathered friends, human and otherwise. It all seems like merrie olde England with grouse, partridge, wild duck, venison, and hare, fish fresh their native habitat; the gastronomic glories that are the British hams and sausages; and the burly butchers educated in the English, American, and painstaking French styles. It is here that variety meats are treated with as much respect as the scarlet-coated lobsters standing guard.

BRITISH BARBECUED KIDNEYS

Beef, veal, lamb, and pork kidneys are superb cooked over the coals. Don't remove the outer fat because it cooks to a crisp as it bastes the kidneys. Split the kidneys about halfway through and remove the cores. Brush with oil, melted butter, or bacon drippings, and grill them over coals about 10 minutes, depending on their size. They should be brown on the outside and still pink and juicy on the inside. Serve with melted butter and wedges of lemon. If you like, you can serve them as part of a mixed grill with chops and sausages.

HUNGARY & FINLAND

The *czardas* or peasant inns were once the hostels for Hungarian cowboys and highwaymen. Today the food is still simple, usually cooked outdoors in a traditional white kiln or over the open fire. The Hungarians cut thick slabs of bacon in coxcomb curls and roast them over the fire for open-faced sandwiches or as the central piece in a mixed grill. Along with the wonderful bacon and sausage, the Hungarian goose liver appears on the epicurean tables of the world and is roasted whole in its own fat over the coals.

TIROLER KALBSLEBER PAPRIKAS
A Skewer of Bacon, Sausages, and Liver

6 thick slices bacon, quartered
6 smoked pork sausages
2 pounds calves liver, cut into 1-1/2-inch pieces
Olive oil
2 tablespoons paprika

Alternate meats on skewers. Brush with oil and sprinkle generously with paprika. Grill over coals, turning and basting with more oil, just until golden and crusty. Liver should be pink inside.
Makes 6 servings

Typical of the dishes served outdoors at the *czardas* is "robber's meat" of mixed pork, veal, and lamb, resting on trestles of fried bread that have been notched to hold the skewers.

RABLO-HUS OF THE CZARDAS
Robber's Meat on Trestles of Fried Bread

1 pound each boneless pork, veal, and lamb
1 teaspoon salt
1/2 teaspoon freshly ground black pepper
1/4 teaspoon cayenne pepper
3 tablespoons grated onion
1 clove garlic, mashed
Bay leaves
2 green bell peppers, cut into squares
2 onions, cut into wedges
Olive oil
Thick slices of bread, fried in olive oil until
    golden, and notched

Cut all meats into 2-inch cubes. Toss in bowl with salt, black pepper, cayenne pepper, grated onion, and garlic. Let stand 1 hour, stirring once or twice. Thread meats on skewers, alternating with bay leaves, green peppers, and onions. Brush with oil. Grill over coals, turning frequently and basting each side with more oil, until nicely browned, about 12 minutes in all. Rest skewers in notches of fried bread.
Makes 6 servings

With a name like Heikki Ratalahti, you have to be my favorite Finn—wry, sly, and marvelously inventive. In response to my query, Heikki came up with an original—sausages cooked over the hot rocks in the sauna. After they are brown and crispy, you simply douse them with a can of beer or icy vodka and the dizzying vapor fills the air.

HEIKKI'S SAUSAGE IN A SAUNA

2 pounds each coarsely ground beef and pork
    trimmings
2 pounds potatoes, peeled, grated, and squeezed
    dry in a towel
2 onions, grated
1 tablespoon each dry mustard and salt
A good pinch each freshly ground pepper,
    ground allspice, and crumbled dried marjoram
Sausage casings
Beer or vodka
Whole-grain bread

Finnish Egg Butter
1/2 pound unsalted butter, softened
4 hard-cooked eggs, finely chopped
Salt and freshly ground pepper to taste
Pinch each freshly grated nutmeg and ground ginger

Mix together the meats, potatoes, onions, and spices. Fill casings loosely and twist into links. Grill sausages over hot rocks in the sauna until nicely browned. Douse with beer or vodka and continue steaming until done. While sausages are cooking, prepare egg butter by kneading together the butter and eggs. Season with spices. Wrap sausages in bread and spread with butter.

The gypsies of Hungary and Yugoslavia fiddled for their supper and sometimes for their lives in the inns of the countryside. Crackling crisp goose with a caraway-scented filling of sauerkraut, prunes, and apples, spitted over an open fire, seems fitting fare for the gypsy in all of us.

PECENA HUSA SE ZELIM
A Crackling Crisp Goose Stuffed with Sauerkraut

1 goose, about 8 pounds
3 medium onions, chopped
3 to 4 pounds sauerkraut, washed, well drained,
    and dried
2 tart green apples, chopped
1 cup pitted prunes, coarsely chopped
1 tablespoon caraway seeds
1 tablespoon paprika
Salt and freshly ground pepper

Remove fat from cavity of goose and render in a skillet. Sauté onions in 2 or 3 tablespoons of the fat. Add sauerkraut and cook 5 minutes more, stirring. Stir in remaining ingredients, adding salt and pepper to taste. Fill cavity and neck of goose with stuffing mixture. Truss openings and balance goose on a spit. Cook 2 to 2-1/2 hours, pricking goose from time to time to release fat.
Makes 6 servings

SOUTHERN EUROPE

ITALY

Marcella Hazan is a treasure of good sense and great cooking. I met up with this charming woman when she was giving cooking classes in the Napa Valley, spelling off from her popular classes in Bologna and from writing cookbooks, among which is her superb *The Classic Italian Cook Book*. She told me: "Cooking over coals is my favorite way of cooking anything and always has been. I grew up in a fishing town where I had fish grilled over charcoal nearly every day. The fishermen used to do it right on the dock when they unloaded their catch. And out in the country, we marinated pork chops or lamb and cooked it over a fire of dried grapevines."

PESCE ALLA MODA DI MARCELLA
Fish Broiled Marcella's Way

2-1/2- to 3-pound whole dressed fish
2 teaspoons salt
1/4 cup olive oil
2 tablespoons fresh lemon juice
Fine, dry bread crumbs
Rosemary, crushed (optional; for use only on
   such dark-fleshed fish as mackerel or bluefish)
1 or 2 bay leaves
Lemon wedges

Salt the fish on both sides and rub with olive oil and lemon juice. Turn the fish in bread crumbs until it is well coated. Add rosemary if you are preparing dark-fleshed fish. Marinate 1 to 2 hours at room temperature. Save the marinade. Toss a bay leaf or two into the fire just before setting the fish on an oiled charcoal grill. Baste the fish occasionally while it grills and turn only once. Cooking times will vary depending on thickness of fish; it should take about 20 minutes. When fish is cooked, the flesh should separate easily from the bone. Serve with lemon wedges.
Makes 4 servings

After pasta, the sea offers the most variety to the Italian cuisine. And since no Italian kitchen is without fresh parsley and coriander, sweet basil, thyme, sage, tarragon, bay, mint, fennel, and saffron, the delicate fish flavor is augmented by a wide spectrum of flavors.

SCAMPI ALLA GRIGLIA
Grilled Shrimp

2 pounds large shrimp in the shell, deveined
1/4 pound unsalted butter, melted
1/2 cup olive oil
1 tablespoon minced shallots or green onion
3 large cloves garlic
1 teaspoon salt
2 tablespoons fresh lemon juice
1/4 cup minced parsley
Salt and freshly ground pepper
Parsley sprigs

Wash shrimp in cold water and dry well. Pour butter and olive oil into a 3-quart shallow bowl. Add shallots. Coarsely chop garlic with salt on a cutting board. (This helps eliminate the strong garlic taste.) Add garlic-salt mixture to bowl. Roll shrimp in this mixture until well coated. Sprinkle with lemon juice and parsley. Marinate at least 30 minutes, turning shrimp several times. Remove shrimp from bowl. Put marinade in a small saucepan and place on the side of the grill. Grill shrimp over coals until they turn pink. Sprinkle shrimp with salt and pepper and serve them in individual scallop shells. Spoon heated marinade over them and garnish with parsley sprigs.
Makes 4 to 6 servings

The Venetians are masters in the art of cooking fish. Nothing is more typically Venetian than the little *trattori* and *rosticceries* along the banks of the canals, where the fish is grilled over fierce charcoal fires.

TRIGLIE SUL FOCONE ALLA VENETO
Venetian Grilled Fish

12 small red mullets or other small fish
Salt and freshly ground pepper
3 bay leaves, broken
1/2 teaspoon crumbled dried thyme
1 tablespoon chopped fresh chives
1 tablespoon chopped parsley
Olive oil

Put fish in shallow casserole. Sprinkle with salt, pepper, and herbs, and drizzle with olive oil. Marinate 1 hour at room temperature, turning occasionally. Cook slowly over coals in wire fish frame, basting frequently with marinade, until fish flakes.
Makes 6 servings

The trenchermen of Italy are the Bolognese, just as the Burgundians are the trenchermen of France. Their food is by far the richest in Italy, the true gastronomic center of the north. "When you hear mention made of Bolognese cooking, drop a little curtsy for it deserves it," wrote Pellegrino Artusi.

POLLO ALLA CONTADINA
Chicken, Country Style

4 small broiler chickens, halved
Salt and freshly ground black pepper
1/8 teaspoon ground cinnamon
Dash of cayenne pepper
1 cup sweet vermouth
3 tablespoons tomato jam or tomato paste
Heavy cream

Put broilers in shallow casserole. Sprinkle with salt, black pepper, cinnamon, and cayenne pepper. Cover with a mixture of vermouth and tomato jam. Marinate 1 hour at room temperature, turning occasionally. Grill over coals, basting with marinade and catching drippings in a drip pan, until chicken is nicely browned, about 30 minutes. Add a little cream and the rest of the marinade to the drippings for a sauce.
Makes 4 servings

The Tuscan restaurants called *girarrosti* (the roasting spit) owe their name to those huge spits, loaded with chickens, pork, suckling kids, guinea fowls, and game of all kinds, from birds to boar, which rotate perpetually over an open fire.

PAETA ARROSTO CON MELAGRANA
Roast Turkey with Pomegranates

8-pound turkey with giblets
Salt and freshly ground pepper
Butter
6 slices bacon
3 pomegranates
Olive oil

Rub cavity of bird with salt, pepper, and butter. Truss openings. Skewer bacon securely over breast. Balance bird on a spit and cook over coals 1 hour, basting with its own juices collected in a drip pan. Meanwhile, roll pomegranates back and forth on a firm surface to release the juice. Cut a small hole in end and pour out juice. Baste turkey with the juice of 2 of the pomegranates. Continue to cook until tender, about 1 hour more.

Prepare a sauce by chopping the giblets and browning them in a little olive oil. Add juice and seeds of remaining pomegranate and heat just to boiling. Serve turkey with the sauce on the side.
Makes 6 servings

Sardinian cuisine is a smidgen of Arab, a touch of African, with lots of Roman innovations.

Sardinia is the land of cooking *a furria furria,* meaning "to turn and turn again." Whole animals —wild boar, suckling pig, baby lambs, young goats —are skinned, cleaned, and spitted on rough rods over a fire of juniper, olive, and mastic trees. The flame must not touch the roast and no herbs are used. As the animal turns, it is impregnated with distinctive aromas and tastes from the wood fire. The Sardinians also use wood fires to cook *a carraxiu,* "in a hole," with myrtle branches.

PORCEDDU ARROSTITO
Roast Suckling Pig

12- to 20-pound dressed suckling pig
Myrtle leaves
1/2-pound piece salt pork (a thick cut)
Salt and freshly ground pepper

Wash and dry the cavity of the pig and rub it well with myrtle leaves. Balance the pig on a spit. Thread the salt pork onto another spit and place over the coals with a pan underneath to catch the drippings, which will be used to baste the pig as it cooks. Start roasting the pig with its flank nearest the fire; then, when the skin is browned, turn it continuously until it is a good rich brown color all over. Sprinkle the pig with salt and pepper and baste it occasionally with the drippings from the salt pork. It will be cooked in 3 to 4 hours.
Makes 8 to 12 servings

The Genoese disdained the spices of far-off lands except as merchandise to be traded for gold. They much preferred the herbs of their own hills to give distinction to their food. The pungency of fresh basil is the soul of the famous *pesto;* the sharpness of sage and rosemary burning over the coals permeates the countryside.

SPIEDINI ALLA GENOVA
Mixed Kabobs, Spoleto Style

6 cubes loin of pork
6 chunks boned chicken breast meat
6 cubes beef liver
6 baby lamb chops
6 slices bacon
Fresh or dried sage and rosemary
Salt and freshly ground pepper
12 juniper berries, crushed
Olive oil

On 6 skewers, interlace the meats with the bacon. Tuck fresh sage leaves and rosemary sprigs between meats (or rub dried herbs over skewered meats). Sprinkle with salt, pepper, crushed juniper berries, and olive oil. Marinate 1 hour at room temperature, turning occasionally. Grill over coals until nicely browned.
Makes 6 servings

Tradition is high among the values of Friuli-Venezia-Giulia, where the center of family life and of the renowned hospitality is the *fogher,* the hearth or open stove. This often stands in the center of the kitchen, with a flared hood above and a beautiful wrought-iron grill from which are hung the spits, pots, and pans.

FEGATO DI VITELLO CON SALVIA
Calves Liver with Sage

1-1/2 pounds beef or calves liver, cut into
   1-1/2-inch cubes
Salt and freshly ground pepper
2 tablespoons chopped fresh sage
1 teaspoon crumbled dried rosemary, or
2 sprigs rosemary, chopped
Juice of 1/2 lemon
Olive oil
6 slices bacon
12 fresh sage leaves

Put liver in shallow dish. Sprinkle with salt and pepper, chopped sage, rosemary, and lemon juice. Drizzle with a little oil. Marinate 1 hour, turning occasionally. Thread on skewers, coiling bacon around cubes and tucking sage leaves between them. Grill, brushing with marinade, until browned but still pink inside.
Makes 4 to 6 servings

The *pilotto* is a piece of lard wrapped in paper, which is then set afire so that the melting fat drips over the meat roasting on a spit. The *ghiotta* is a dish that is placed under the spit to collect the fat that drips from the meat. White wine, vinegar, lemon, sage, and black olives are piled in the *ghiotta,* and as the hot fat drips into this it releases an aromatic vapor, which seasons the meat above. In this recipe, the skewered meat is rolled in herbs that toast to a char over the hot coals. The skewer is then wrapped in grilled prosciutto.

AGNELLO ALLA GHIOTTA
Lamb with Aromatic Herbs

5-1/2- to 6-pound leg of lamb, boned, trimmed,
   and cut into 1-1/2-inch cubes
1/2 pound bacon, cut into very thin 1-inch-long
   strips
4 green bell peppers, seeded and cut into squares
Peanut oil
Dry aromatic herb mixture of crushed thyme,
   bay leaf, sage, rosemary, and summer savory
16 very thin slices prosciutto

Thread lamb cubes onto skewers alternately with the bacon and green pepper pieces. Brush with oil and roll in the herb mixture. Grill over coals, turning once, a few minutes on each side until nicely browned. Meanwhile, grill the slices of prosciutto. Wrap 1 slice around each skewer on the bias before serving.
Makes 8 servings

Next to *porchetta,* the Roman countryside is blanketed with woolly sheep and suckling lamb, the most famous of which is *abbacchio.* The baby is killed when it is only three weeks old. It is spitted with *strutto,* matured pork fat, and garlic, sage, and rosemary. Just before serving, it is seasoned with anchovy paste.

ABBACCHIO ALLA ROMANA
Lamb, Roman Style

12- to 20-pound dressed suckling lamb
8 cloves garlic, crushed
Fresh chopped sage and rosemary
Salt and freshly ground pepper
Pork fat in sheets
2 tablespoons anchovy paste

With a sharp knife, make deep incisions in lamb. Make a paste of garlic and herbs and poke into incisions with your fingers. Season with salt and pepper. Tie sheets of pork fat over top and sides. Balance lamb on spit and roast 2-1/2 to 3 hours until juicy pink. Rub with anchovy paste and carve.
Makes 8 to 12 servings

Other baby lamb dishes favored by the Romans are "burn-your-fingers-chops" because they are cooked on a grill and turned over with the fingers.

COSTOLETTE A COSTADITI
Burn-Your-Fingers Chops

12 baby lamb chops, 1-1/2 inches thick
Salt and freshly ground pepper
1 clove garlic, mashed with
2 anchovy fillets
2 tablespoons olive oil
2 green bell peppers

Season lamb chops with salt and pepper. Combine garlic-anchovy mixture with oil and rub into chops. Let stand at room temperature about 1 hour. Cut peppers into chunks and thread on skewers. Set skewers and chops on grill over coals and cook quickly.
Makes 4 servings

The task of the Tuscan cook is not an easy one. His dishes of classic simplicity—his *bistecca alla fiorentina,* for example—are essentially a rite. The cut of beef must be of just the right size and thickness, from just the right animal (the *vitellone,* no longer a calf but not yet an ox). At the last minute, while the meat is still on the heat, after being seasoned with salt and pepper, it is brushed with the finest Tuscan olive oil.

BISTECCHE ALLA FIORENTINA
Steak, Tuscan Style

3-pound prime T-bone steak, cut at least
   1 inch thick
Salt and freshly ground pepper
Fine Tuscan olive oil
Lemon wedges

Ask your butcher for a well-aged cut from a young steer. Grill over coals to desired doneness. While steak is still over the coals, season with salt and pepper and brush with olive oil. Serve with lemon wedges.
Makes 6 servings

THE HERB BASTING OIL OF LUCCA

Pour 2 cups good Italian olive oil into a bottle or jar with a tight-fitting lid. Drop in 2 or 3 cloves of garlic, a dried hot red chili pepper, crushed, a few crushed peppercorns, and one or more of the following:
Sage leaves, fresh or dried
Rosemary sprigs
Oregano sprigs
Sprigs of fennel feathers or fennel seeds, crushed
Juniper berries, crushed

"To dress a Peacocke with all his feathers, in such sort that when it is enough it shall seem to bee alive and call fire out of the mouth . . . And to make the greater show, when the Peacocke is roasted you may gild it with leafe gold, put the skin upon said gold, which may be spiced very sweet. The like may be done with a Feesant, or other fowl." Epulario, *Giovanni de' Rosselli*

SPAIN & PORTUGAL

The Basque nature is not to be different, but only to excel. The Basque cooking is not the most imaginative; it is simply the best. A famous specialty is the Navarrese trout, which were originally caught by the shepherds tending their flocks near the icy streams. The trout are rubbed, inside and out, with the fat from chunks of serrano ham (or stuffed with thin slices of the ham) and grilled quickly over fires of rosemary and thyme branches.

TRUCHAS A LA NAVARRESE
Navarrese Trout

1/4 pound thinly sliced serrano ham or prosciutto, or any smoked ham
Olive oil
4 large trout
Salt and freshly ground pepper
Rosemary and thyme branches or the herbs dried
Browned butter flavored with fresh lemon juice

Trim fat from the ham and rub fat with a little olive oil. Rub trout, inside and out, with fat. Fold a slice of ham neatly into cavity of fish. Sprinkle fish with salt and pepper and let stand 30 minutes. Arrange trout on branches of herbs in hinged grill (or toss a handful of herbs into the coals) and grill about 3 minutes to a side. Serve with browned butter sharpened with lemon juice.
Makes 4 servings

At the great fish auctions in Spain and Portugal, the splashes of color are so intense, the actions and sounds so theatric, you feel as though you are in some strange aquarium. Although this is not a traditional *zarzuela de mariscos,* I have adapted it because it translates beguilingly as a "light operetta of seafood."

ZARZUELA DE MARISCOS
"A Light Operetta of Seafood"

2 pounds assorted firm, fresh fish fillets, cut into chunks with skin left on
2 pounds large shrimp in the shell
1 or 2 cloves garlic, crushed and mixed with
Approximately 1/3 cup olive oil
1 quart mussels
1/2 cup dry white wine
Pinch of saffron threads
1 large onion, finely chopped
1 large tomato, peeled and finely chopped
2 cloves garlic, crushed
3 tablespoons crushed toasted almonds
Salt and freshly ground pepper to taste

Alternate fish and shrimp on skewers and brush with garlic-flavored oil. In a covered saucepan simmer mussels with all remaining ingredients just until mussels are tender, about 5 to 8 minutes.

Grill skewered seafood over coals until nicely browned, about 4 minutes on each side, basting with the oil. Set skewers of fish in bowls and spoon mussels and sauce over all.
Makes 8 servings

My good, neighborly friend, Shirley Sarvis, covered all of Portugal in her quest for *A Taste of Portugal.* She described to me one of her favorite dishes—cod cooked over the coals. This is the fish the Portuguese could live on the rest of their lives—not only possible, but practical.

Passing the oil and vinegar is not incidental to this dish; it is fundamental. The proper potatoes with this are punched potatoes, roasted in the same coals that cook the cod. Baking the cod after barbecuing allows it to absorb the oil it needs.

BACALHAU ASSADO NA BRASA
Cod Roasted in Embers

4 thick slices salt cod, about 1-1/2 pounds
Olive oil
2 large cloves garlic, minced or crushed
1 large sweet onion, finely chopped
Approximately 1/2 cup pitted green olives
6 hard-cooked eggs, sliced
Olive oil and white wine vinegar

Soak cod in cold water for 24 to 48 hours, until very moist. Change water two or three times, drain well, and remove skin and bones.

Brush cod with oil and grill over coals until barely charred on both sides, basting with more oil. Arrange slices in shallow platter and spoon over about 1/2 cup olive oil mixed with the garlic. Bake in a slow oven (300°) for 10 to 15 minutes. Sprinkle with onion and garnish with olives and eggs. Pass olive oil and vinegar.
Makes 4 servings

Murro means punch, and you punch these potatoes when they come out of the coals. The salt-crusted skins break and the mealy inside puffs out.

Potatoes old enough to have thick skins will break in one place and open when dealt a blow; new potatoes are likely just to mash. Roast these potatoes at the edge of coals while cooking any meat or fish.

BATATAS A MURRO
Punched Potatoes

Baking potatoes, about 2-1/2 inches in diameter
Lard
Coarse salt

Rub potatoes with lard and roll in salt to coat. Place potatoes alongside low-glowing coals. Roast for about 1 hour or until tender, turning occasionally. Break the skin of each potato ("smash with hands," reads the recipe translation) and pinch at bottom so inside puffs out.

SALMON AL HORNO
Salmon with Sherry

6 salmon steaks, about 1 inch thick
1/2 cup medium-dry sherry
1/2 cup olive oil
1 tablespoon red wine vinegar
1 teaspoon salt
Chopped anise or fennel feathers (or use a good
   pinch of the dried)
1 cup pimiento-stuffed olives, sliced

Marinate salmon steaks for several hours in mixture of all remaining ingredients, except olives. Pat steaks dry. Grill over coals until lightly charred on both sides. Spoon olives and a bit of marinade over each serving.
Makes 6 servings

The Spanish equivalent of the French *aioli* or garlic mayonnaise is *ali-oli,* tinted a sunset pink with pimiento. It is most often served with a Catalonian sauce called *romescu,* which has a sharp, quick flavor that makes your mouth water for grilled shellfish and meats. Serve both sauces. I like a big dab of one on top of the other.

PERFECTLY COOKED SHRIMP
OVER THE COALS

Wrap large shrimp in the shell individually in wet grape leaves or foil. Cook over the coals for 10 to 15 minutes, depending on size, turning once or twice. Serve with Ali-oli and Romescu sauces, following.

ALI-OLI
Garlic Mayonnaise

1 canned pimiento
4 to 8 cloves garlic
1 cup olive oil
1 egg
1 tablespoon fresh lemon juice
Salt

In a blender whirl pimiento and garlic with 1/4 cup of the oil until smooth. Add egg and blend. With the motor running, slowly add rest of oil in a thin, steady stream until mixture holds its shape. Add lemon juice and salt to taste.
Makes approximately 1-1/2 cups

CATALONIAN ROMESCU
Almond and Hot Pepper Sauce

1/4 cup toasted almonds
1 clove garlic, crushed
1/2 teaspoon crushed hot red pepper or
   Tabasco sauce
1 small tomato, peeled and seeded
1 cup olive oil
Red wine vinegar
Salt

In a blender grind almonds with garlic, red pepper, tomato, and a tablespoon or so of the oil to make a paste. With the motor running, slowly add rest of oil in a thin, steady stream until mixture holds its shape. Add vinegar and salt to taste.
Makes approximately 1-1/2 cups

The ancestral Basque homesteads in the Pyrénées near San Sebastian gave rise to the cuisine of *Las Vascongadas*. Any menu item in a reputable restaurant followed by *a la vasca, a la vasconia, a la vizcaina, a la vascongada* means it is in the Basque manner and is well worth its salt. This sauce of charcoal-roasted vegetables, called *chilindrón*, might well be the world's best "barbecue" sauce.

POLLO A LA CHILINDRÓN
Chicken with Peppers, Onions, Tomatoes, and Olives

2 large onions
2 green bell peppers
2 fresh hot chili peppers
6 tomatoes
1/2 pound serrano ham or prosciutto, or any smoked ham, cut into chunks
6 each pitted green and black olives, cut in half
Salt and freshly ground pepper to taste
Sugar
6 whole chicken breasts
Lemon wedges

Skewer vegetables and ham separately and cook over coals, turning until nicely charred. Put vegetables in a paper bag to "sweat," then rub off the skins. Coarsely chop vegetables and put into a saucepan with the ham. Cook briskly until sauce is thick. Add olives and seasonings. Brush chicken with sauce and grill over coals, turning and basting until nicely charred. Serve chicken with rest of sauce, kept hot on side of grill. Serve with wedges of lemon.
Makes 6 servings

The wonderful sight and smell of little birds twirling on spits before glowing "fire walls" is as common in Spain as in New York, where they are cooked on electric rotisseries. *Pollo al ast* is a Spanish fad, and there are even little bird bars where you can drop in and munch on a partridge or a chicken.

PERDIZ SABRE CANAPE A LA MESONERA
Flamed Birds

4 little game birds with livers
1/2 cup each chopped cooked ham and garlic sausage
1/4 cup olive oil
1 cup soft bread crumbs
1 cup seedless grapes
Salt and freshly ground pepper
Butter
Paprika
Oloroso or cream sherry
1/4 cup brandy, warmed in a small pan placed on the grill
Toasted bread rounds

Sauté livers with ham and sausage in oil. Add bread crumbs and grapes. Season with salt and pepper. Stuff birds and truss openings. Rub birds with butter and sprinkle with salt and paprika. Balance on a spit or set in a smoke oven and cook, basting with sherry, until nicely browned. Flame birds with brandy just before serving. Serve on toasted bread rounds.
Makes 4 servings

POLLO FRITO AL JEREZ
"Fried Chicken"

3- to 4-pound chicken, cut into serving pieces
1/3 cup dry Spanish sherry
A good pinch of paprika
2 teaspoons each ground cumin, salt, sugar, and
   white vinegar
2 cloves garlic, crushed

Marinate chicken in a mixture of all remaining ingredients at room temperature for 1 hour or so. Grill chicken over coals until crisp and charred, but still moist on the inside.
Makes 4 servings

The succulent pigs of Old Castile taste of the barley and thyme and other wild herbs their mothers have been feeding on. The piglet himself has not tasted anything but milk—and since he was dedicated to St. Anthony, he has been blessed and showered with holy water to fatten him while his fat father goes to the slaughterhouse.

CARNE DE PORCO CON VINHA D'ALHOS
Portuguese Ribcage in a Wine of Garlic

4 pounds country-style spareribs, in 1 piece
2 cups dry white wine
1/2 cup white wine vinegar
2 tablespoons olive oil
6 cloves garlic, crushed
1 tablespoon each coriander seeds and
   cumin seeds, crushed

Trim fat from ribs and set ribs in shallow glass baking pan. Mix together rest of ingredients and pour over pork. Marinate up to 4 days in the refrigerator, turning twice a day. Grill ribs over coals until nicely browned, about 20 minutes to a side, basting with marinade as they cook.
Makes 4 servings·

Paintings in the ancient caves of northern Spain were part of a ritual before the all-important hunt. The animals depicted were usually those fitted for food.

The bullfighter's steak of Spain, marinated in a fruity olive oil with chunks of orange and lemon, is a big chuck steak from the tender end. The bullfighter's steak of Portugal is different. They do not kill the bulls at the bullfights there, so they simply squeeze a lemon over their fillets cooked on charcoal braziers around the bull rings.

CADERA DE TORO
Bullfighter's Steak

3-pound chuck steak, cut from tender end
1/2 cup olive oil
1 lemon, quartered
1 orange, quartered
2 cloves garlic, crushed
2 whole cloves
2 bay leaves
Salt and freshly ground pepper to taste

Slash steak all over with a sharp knife. Heat oil, add rest of ingredients and simmer gently until fruit is lightly browned. Pour over meat and let marinate at room temperature 4 hours or more. Grill over coals slowly, until desired doneness.
Makes 4 to 6 servings

You must drink Asturian cider quickly for it is the foam that counts. It sparkles and tickles your throat. The cider is poured from the bottle with a straight arm from high over the head, while the glass is held close to the floor. It is used in place of wine in much of the cooking and is an excellent marinade for the thick veal steaks of the region, which are traditionally served with two fried eggs on a bed of grilled potatoes, surrounded by a bed of rice, and garnished with pitted black olives.

CHULETAS DE TERUENA A LA JULIANCHU
Charcoal-grilled Veal Steaks

4 veal steaks, about 2 inches thick
1/2 cup olive oil
1 tablespoon fresh lemon juice
2 cloves garlic, crushed
Chopped fresh mint
1/2 cup apple cider

Punch holes in the steaks with a thick skewer. Combine rest of ingredients in a bowl and marinate meat at room temperature 2 hours or more. Pat dry. Grill over coals until nicely browned, about 10 minutes on each side for lightly pink, juicy veal.
Makes 4 servings

In the hot, humming streets of Spain, the smell of spicy sausages grilling over the open fires is constant. The small Andalusian town of Jabugo is famous for its *chorizos,* stuffed and tied by the women, then hung on rafters and left to smoke over constantly burning little fires of encina or evergreen oak.

BASQUE CHORIZOS

4-1/2 pounds boneless pork
1 pound boneless beef chuck
1/2 pound pork fat
6 dried sweet chili peppers, seeds removed
1/2 cup hot water
3 cloves garlic, crushed
1 tablespoon salt
1 teaspoon freshly ground pepper
2 teaspoons paprika
1/4 cup dry red wine
Sausage casings

Put meats and fat through coarse blade of a meat grinder. Cover chilies with hot water to soften, about 15 minutes. Whirl chilies with water in a blender until smooth. Mix meats with chilies and rest of ingredients. Cover and chill overnight. Fill sausage casings and tie. Simmer sausages, covered, in a little water for 10 minutes before grilling over coals.
Makes approximately 6 pounds

Typical of the imaginative uses of chorizo are these little "mock partridges" of veal and ham rolled up with herbs and tied with string. It is sporting to spear them on green sticks and roast them over the coals for a perfectly sensational Basque hot dog.

PERDICES DEL CAPELLAN
Little Mock Partridges

6 thin slices veal
6 thin slices ham
12 thin slices chorizo or other smoked sausage
Butter mixed with chopped fresh thyme and
    minced garlic to taste
Olive oil

Pound each veal slice thin, then pound edges of a ham slice into each veal slice with the flat edge of a cleaver. Arrange 2 slices sausage on each. Spread with herb butter. Roll up and tie with string. Impale each on a stick or long-handled fork and brown slowly and evenly over the coals, basting with oil as they cook.
Makes 6 servings

Since dunking and mopping is a necessary ritual in the Spanish cuisine, here are three good sauces, each with a splash of sherry, to use at your outdoor feasts.

SALSA COLORADO
Red Sauce

2 cloves garlic, crushed
2 canned pimientos, well drained
1 slice white bread, crusts removed
1/4 cup olive oil
1/4 cup dry Spanish sherry
Salt and freshly ground pepper

Whirl garlic with pimiento in a blender. Soak bread in a little water and squeeze dry. Add bread to garlic mixture. Beat in oil, a drop at a time, until sauce is thick. Thin with wine, blending until smooth. Season to taste with salt and pepper.
Makes approximately 1/2 cup

SALSA VERDE
Green Sauce

1 cup parsley sprigs
2 cloves garlic
1/4 cup olive oil
Salt
Fresh lemon juice
Spanish sherry

Finely mince parsley and garlic in a blender, adding oil a bit at a time until sauce is thick and pungent. Season to taste with salt, lemon juice, and sherry.
Makes approximately 1/2 cup

SALSA AMARILLA
Yellow Sauce

6 hard-cooked eggs
2 tablespoons olive oil
2 tablespoons Spanish sherry
1 teaspoon dry mustard
Grated zest and juice of 1 lemon
Salt and freshly ground pepper

Separate whites from yolks. Mash yolks smooth, beating in oil drop by drop until creamy. Add sherry, mustard, and lemon juice and zest. Mince egg whites and fold in. Season to taste with salt and pepper.
Makes approximately 1 cup

THE MIDDLE EAST & AFRICA

A GREEK FISH, STUFFED, CHARRED IN GRAPE LEAVES

1/4 cup each finely chopped Greek olives
   and onion
2 tablespoons olive oil
2 slices cold boiled ham, chopped
1/4 cup finely chopped fresh herbs, such as
   parsley, oregano, and/or thyme
1 egg, lightly beaten
Dash each salt and freshly ground pepper
3- to 4-pound whole dressed red snapper or
   other fatty fish
4 thin slices lemon
Grape leaves
2 tablespoons butter

Lightly mix olives, onion, oil, ham, herbs, egg, and salt and pepper for stuffing. Pat evenly into fish cavity and line with lemon slices. Wrap the fish in a double thickness of wet grape leaves (or in foil or parchment). Grill over coals about 20 minutes on each side, turning once. Unwrap and place fish on a hot platter and add butter to juices collected in wrapping. Season with salt and pepper and spoon over fish.
Makes 4 servings

FISH WITH ORANGE AND LEMON SLICES, GREEK STYLE

3- to 3-1/2-pound whole dressed firm-fleshed fish
Salt and freshly ground pepper
4 thin slices each orange and lemon
3 oranges, peeled and sectioned
Rosemary or parsley sprigs (optional)

Sprinkle inside of fish with salt and pepper; arrange orange and lemon slices inside fish. Place fish in hinged grill and cook over coals, turning once, until fish easily flakes with a fork, about 20 minutes on each side. Serve with orange sections and garnish with rosemary sprigs.
Makes 4 servings

Everybody says the best fish in Baghdad is *mas-goof*—cooked over the coals on the banks of the Tigris River. The fish stalls feature your choice of any number of varieties, seasoned with rock salt and paprika, impaled on sticks, and arranged in a circle around the crackling twigs. You must eat the fish with your fingers "so you can feel the bones."

FISH WITH FENNEL

1/2 cup olive oil
1 teaspoon each crumbled dried fennel and thyme
2 tablespoons minced parsley
2 tablespoons dry white wine or fresh lemon juice
1 tablespoon anise-flavored liqueur
3-pound whole dressed bluefish, striped bass,
   or perch

Combine olive oil, fennel, thyme, parsley, wine, and liqueur. Make 2 slanting incisions on each side of fish and coat fish with marinade. Grill fish over coals, turning once, until flesh flakes easily, about 15 minutes to a side.
Makes 6 servings

An ancient Greek method for broiling lean fish was to immerse it in enough salted olive oil to cover (one teaspoon sea salt to one cup oil). The oil does wonderful things for both texture and flavor. I do this with lean lamb and beef as well as fish.

FISH IN THE STYLE OF ATHENAEUS
Fish Grilled on Bay Leaves

6 halibut or flounder steaks, 1 inch thick
Olive oil
Sea salt
Grape or fig leaves
Bay leaves and parsley sprigs
Ground cumin, salt, and freshly ground pepper
Chopped fresh oregano, capers, and lemon wedges

Place fish in a shallow dish and pour over just enough olive oil mixed with salt to cover. Marinate at room temperature 1 hour or so. Arrange grape leaves in a hinged grill and top with bay leaves and several sprigs of parsley. Set drained fish on top and sprinkle lightly with cumin, salt, and pepper. Top with grape leaves and close grill. Cook over coals about 4 to 6 minutes on each side. Grape leaves will be charred. Serve with bowls of oregano, capers, and lemon wedges.
Makes 6 servings

TAS KEBAB
Chicken Kabobs

2 whole chicken breasts, split, skinned, boned, and
   cut into 2-inch pieces
2 green bell peppers, cut into 1-inch pieces
2 large tomatoes, cut into wedges
1/4 cup fresh lemon juice
3 tablespoons butter or margarine, melted
1 teaspoon paprika
1/2 teaspoon salt
1/4 teaspoon cayenne pepper

Place chicken, green peppers, and tomatoes in a
medium-sized bowl. Mix together all remaining ingredients and pour over chicken and vegetables.
Toss gently to coat. Cover and let stand at room
temperature for 1 hour. Thread chicken, green
peppers, and tomatoes alternately onto 4 skewers.
Grill over coals, turning and basting with remaining
marinade, until chicken is tender, about 15 to 20
minutes.
Makes 4 servings

So many Lebanese dishes are spiced with cinnamon, paprika, and cayenne pepper that most cooks
have a shaker pre-mixed.

PEDABURGERS

Spice Mix
1-1/2 teaspoons each ground cinnamon, paprika,
   and salt
1/2 teaspoon cayenne pepper

3 pounds lean ground lamb
1/2 cup plain yogurt
1 cup chopped onions
1/2 cup chopped tomatoes, drained
1/4 cup chopped fresh mint
Salt and freshly ground pepper
8 peda bread, warmed on grill and split

Combine ingredients for spice mix. Combine lamb
with yogurt and spice mix and shape into 8 patties.
Grill over coals until browned but still pink, about
8 to 10 minutes altogether. Meanwhile, mix onions, tomatoes, mint, and salt and pepper to taste.
Spoon into split peda bread with lamb patties.
Makes 8 servings

SIS KEBAB
Turkish Lamb Kabobs

1-1/2 pounds lamb from leg, cut into 1-1/2-inch
   cubes
2 green bell peppers, cut into 1-inch pieces
2 red bell peppers, cut into 1-inch pieces
3 tablespoons fresh lemon juice
2 tablespoons olive oil
1 medium onion, grated
1/2 teaspoon salt
1/4 teaspoon crumbled dried thyme
1/8 teaspoon freshly ground pepper

Place lamb and peppers in a medium-sized bowl. Mix together remaining ingredients and pour over lamb and peppers. Toss gently to coat. Cover and let stand at room temperature for 1 hour. Thread lamb and peppers alternately onto 4 skewers. Grill over coals, turning occasionally, until nicely browned, about 5 minutes to a side.
Makes 4 servings

In Greece, street vendors offer bite-sized cubes of marinated meat grilled on skewers, which are served with chunks of bread—split—on sticks. You pull off the bread, wrap it around the meat, and eat it as you walk.

ARNI SOUVLAKIA — *Excellent*
(butterfly leg)

2 pounds lamb from leg, cut into 1-1/2-inch cubes
1/4 cup each olive oil and fresh lemon juice
1 large onion, cut into wedges
2 bay leaves
2 teaspoons crumbled dried oregano
1 teaspoon salt
A grind of pepper

Marinate lamb with rest of ingredients 1 to 2 hours. String on skewers with onions. Grill over coals until nicely browned but still pink inside, about 5 minutes to a side.
Makes 6 servings

Doner kebab (*schawarma* in Lebanon) is a festival dish made up of an elaborate layering of marinated meat slices on a giant spit that slowly turns on a vertical grill. The chef carves off thin, crispy slices and deftly arranges them on split peda bread. This is an adaptation that almost tastes like the real thing.

TURKISH DONER KEBAB

5- to 6-pound leg of lamb with bone

Basting Sauce
1/2 cup each olive oil and red wine vinegar
2 tablespoons fresh lemon juice
1 onion, finely chopped
2 cloves garlic, crushed
1/2 teaspoon each salt, freshly grated nutmeg,
 ground ginger, and freshly ground pepper
Pinch of ground cloves

Yogurt Sauce
2 cups plain yogurt
1/2 cup well-drained grated cucumber
1/4 cup finely chopped fresh mint
1 clove garlic, crushed
Salt and freshly ground pepper

Peda bread, warmed on grill and split

Combine ingredients for basting sauce. Balance meat on a spit and roast 1 hour, basting often until brown and crusty. While meat is cooking, combine ingredients for yogurt sauce. Remove meat from barbecue but not from spit, and slice off crusty thin slices with pink meat for peda bread sandwiches with yogurt sauce. Return leg to barbecue and continue roasting and basting until brown and crusty again—and again.
Makes 8 to 10 servings

"Salam 'Alaikum . . . Wa A'laikum As-Salam"
In 1977 P. Iseman wrote "The Arabian past is too harsh, the future too seductive." Yet the roast mutton kabobs and lamb sarma are still without peer. But the ultimate comment in response to a contemporary question by John Gunther: "Will the jeep ever replace the camel?" When the jeep dies one cannot use it for the meat in a tribal feast.

In ancient Persia the yogurt was beaten with fresh spring water for a foamy drink like an ice cream soda, or it was mixed with onion and saffron as a tart marinade for lamb. Yogurt with diced cucumbers and chopped fresh dill is such a national standby in Turkey that it has been dubbed "Turquoise."

KEBAB BARG
Persian Lamb Kabobs

5-pound leg of lamb, boned and sliced
   1/2 inch thick
1 large onion, grated
3 cups plain yogurt
1/16 teaspoon powdered saffron (optional)
Salt and freshly ground pepper

Cut sliced lamb in strips 2 inches wide and about 5 inches long. Mix onion with yogurt and saffron. Put lamb in yogurt marinade; refrigerate, covered, 2 hours or so. Thread each piece of meat on 2 thin skewers, running them lengthwise through long edges of the meat. Sprinkle with salt and pepper, and grill over coals about 4 minutes to a side.

This is generally served with a buttered rice called *chello*. Each serving of rice has embedded in its conically shaped top a raw egg yolk in half an egg shell.
Makes 8 servings

The rotisserie restaurant of Greece is called the *psistarya*, a meeting and eating place where Greek comedies and tragedies are everyday happenings. By dawn on Easter Sunday the whole country is shrouded in a haze of gray from the communal roasting pits. The innards of the lamb are used to make the Easter sausage, *kokoretsi*. They are speared on a skewer, bound with lamb intestine, and roasted over the coals to be passed around while the lamb dances on the spit.

ROAST LAMB OVER GRAPEVINE CUTTINGS

Have your butcher dress a young lamb, or use a short-cut leg of lamb weighing 5 to 6 pounds. Balance meat on a spit or set in a smoke oven. Grapevine cuttings and a few cloves of garlic tossed on the coals create a distinctive smoke. Baste lamb with a mixture of equal parts clarified butter and olive oil to which cloves of crushed garlic have been added. Use a basting brush of rosemary, thyme, and bay branches. Cook lamb until meat thermometer registers 140° to 150°F. Serve with a fresh mint chutney made by chopping a generous handful of fresh mint leaves and combining them with an equal amount of chopped onion. Stir in a little chopped tomato and season to taste with fresh lemon juice and honey.
Makes 6 to 16 servings, depending on meat used

A brief lesson in Arab table manners: First, the ceremonial washing of hands, then grace is said. The only utensil put before you on the floor (which is where you are, for nomads travel light and chairless) is a huge communal dish. The food must be eaten with your right hand, preferably with your first three fingers. Pluck the meat from the bones, grasp a handful of rice and squeeze it lightly into a ball, smack your lips, and give one well-rounded belch as proof that you have eaten well. Praise Allah again and wash your hands.

ARABIAN SMOKED STUFFED PEPPERS

6 large red or green bell peppers
3 tablespoons olive oil
1 large onion, minced
2 tomatoes, peeled and chopped
2 cloves garlic, crushed
1 pound lean ground lamb
1/2 cup pine nuts
1 teaspoon each crumbled dried marjoram and
   summer savory
1 cup soft bread crumbs
Salt and freshly ground pepper
Olive oil for basting

Cut a 1-inch slice from the top of each pepper. Pull out seeds and membranes and set peppers aside. In a large skillet heat oil and add onion, tomatoes, garlic, and lamb. Cook, stirring, until lamb is grayish; then add rest of ingredients. Spoon stuffing lightly into peppers. Brush tops with more olive oil. Set peppers on a double thickness of foil in a smoke oven; cook 30 minutes or until tender.
Makes 6 servings

The Balkans are famous for their skewered charcoal grills and each region has its very own style. Among the Yugoslavian grilled meats, *cevapcici*, are meatballs ground very fine and kneaded like dough; meat patties of veal and pork, veal, lamb; and pork kabobs. The meat is roasted on square grills over branches of grapevines and charcoal. Near the Albanian border where Oriental customs are strong, they put small pieces of hard mountain cheese on spits for toasting over the coals to be eaten with warm bread and milk.

CEVAPCICI OF YUGOSLAVIA
Fine Textured Meatballs of Lamb and Beef

1 pound each ground lamb and beef
2 medium onions, finely chopped
1 clove garlic, finely chopped
1 egg, lightly beaten
2 teaspoons salt
1/4 teaspoon freshly ground pepper
4 teaspoons paprika
2 tablespoons lard, melted

Thoroughly mix ground meats with *half* of the chopped onion and all the remaining ingredients. Shape cylinders (about 2 inches long and 1 inch in diameter) around skewers, fitting 3 or 4 on each skewer. Chill 1 hour or more, to solidify. Grill over coals until very brown on all sides. Serve, sprinkled with remaining chopped onion.
Makes 6 servings

The pomegranate is the stained-glass window of Middle Eastern cuisine. Its seeds glow rosily in green salads, nutty grains. Its juices are used for marinating lamb and tinting creamy desserts and confections. The best way to deal with a pomegranate is to slice it in half, put one of the halves cut side down in the palm of your left hand, and give it several good whacks with the blunt side of a knife. You'll have a handful of beautiful seeds.

SPITTED LAMB AND BEEF ROLL

2 cups olive oil
1 cup fresh lemon juice
1 lemon, finely chopped
2 medium onions, grated
6 cloves garlic, crushed
1 tablespoon each salt and paprika
1 teaspoon cumin seeds
1 teaspoon cracked peppercorns
Seeds from 1 pomegranate
4-1/2- to 5-pound boneless leg of lamb, rolled and
    tied around 1- to 1-1/2-pound piece boneless
    sirloin steak
Watercress sprigs, kumquats, and lemon slices for
    garnish (optional)

Combine all ingredients except meat and garnishes, and pour over meat. Refrigerate, covered, turning occasionally, 3 days. Let meat stand 2 hours at room temperature before roasting. Then balance meat on a spit and roast, basting occasionally with marinade, until thermometer registers 135° to 145°F for medium rare. Garnish with watercress, kumquats, and lemon slices.
Makes 8 to 10 servings

Marco Polo noted that the Tartar kahns had replaced the Persian shahs as the mightiest of the Oriental rulers. The Tartars were a different breed. They ate fresh-killed raw meat or placed a hunk of meat underneath their saddles to be cooked by "friction" as they galloped across the steppes.

STEAK WITH STEAK TARTARE

4 boneless loin strip steaks, about 1 inch thick
1 pound very lean, coarsely ground beef
1 cup finely chopped parsley
1/2 cup chopped green onions
1 tablespoon capers
2 tablespoons brandy
Salt and freshly ground pepper to taste

Butterfly the steaks, taking care not to cut all the way through. Mix together rest of ingredients. Spread thickly on one half of the cut side of each steak. Press cut sides together and grill over coals, about 5 minutes for each side. No sense doing this number if your guests don't like tartare steak, and that means *raw*.
Makes 4 to 8 servings

*In supplication to a "Yul-lha" or "God of this place,"
the Tartar tribesman rides his sturdy pony through the
consecrated smoke of a juniper fire before launching
onto the plains and steppes with a cut of raw meat under
his saddle to render it tender . . .
Hence the possible origin of "steak tartare."*

Most Middle Easterners disdain the use of anything but salt and pepper on their roasted lamb and mutton. The long marinating durations are throwbacks to the days when refrigeration was not available and the marinade was used to preserve the meat and, perhaps, to disguise its gamy flavor. Mideast hamburgers—*kofta* in Turkey, *kafta* in Lebanon—are grilled and served inside peda, Arab pocket bread.

TURKISH BEEF OR LAMB KOFTA

2 pounds lean ground beef or lamb
1-1/2 cups finely chopped onions
1 small bunch parsley, finely chopped
2 teaspoons salt
1/2 teaspoon each ground cinnamon, paprika, and cayenne pepper
8 peda bread, warmed on grill and split

Mix beef, onion, parsley, and spices until well blended. Shape into 8 patties. Set on a well-greased grill or in a hinged grill and cook over coals to desired doneness, about 10 minutes altogether for rare. Slip patties into peda bread.
Makes 8 servings

KOFTA SKEWERED WITH EGGPLANT

Prepare *kofta* as for patties, preceding. Chill. Use small Japanese eggplants, if you can find them, or regular eggplants, cut into 2-inch cubes. Roll meat into 1-1/2-inch balls and thread on greased skewers with eggplant, pressing together firmly. Brush with olive oil flavored with crushed garlic. Sprinkle with salt and freshly ground pepper as they cook over the coals, about 15 to 20 minutes.
Makes 8 servings

According to an ancient Persian myth, the earth is supported on one horn of a bull, and every year the bull switches horns to gain a little relief from his load. A grouping of eggs rests on a mirror and begins to jiggle as the bull shifts over to the new year at hand. A thirteen-day celebration follows, spring has sprung, and day-long picnics begin. There are skewered kabobs of lamb and sturgeon, joints of chicken marinated in lemon juice, melons and peaches, and exotic sherbets.

A PERSIAN GALA WITH STEAK AND EGGPLANT

Sauce
2 egg yolks
2 tablespoons white wine vinegar
1 tablespoon fresh lemon juice
4 large cloves garlic
1 teaspoon salt
3/4 cup olive oil
1/2 cup finely ground toasted almonds

4 beef fillet steaks, about 2 inches thick
1 large eggplant, unpeeled and cut lengthwise into thin slices
2 tablespoons each melted butter and olive oil
12 cooked artichoke hearts

Put egg yolks, vinegar, lemon juice, garlic, and salt in a blender. Blend at low speed, gradually adding oil in a fine steady stream until sauce is as thick as mayonnaise. Spoon into bowl and fold in almonds. Brush steaks and eggplant slices with mixture of butter and oil. Grill steaks over coals until cooked to desired doneness. Grill eggplant on both sides until lightly charred. Arrange steaks on eggplant slices. Garnish with artichoke hearts and top with a heaping spoonful of the sauce.
Makes 4 servings

AFRICA

Nowhere in Africa is European culture so tenacious as in Portugal's two huge former possessions of Angola and Mozambique. The *piripiri* or hot pepper dishes are Mozambique's favorite feasts—garnished with jacaranda and flamelike plants that seem as full of fire as the food.

CARNARAO GRELHADO PIRIPIRI
The Marinated Prawns of Mozambique

12 jumbo shrimp in the shell
1/4 cup corn oil
1 tablespoon crushed hot red pepper
2 cloves garlic
1 teaspoon salt

Put shrimp in a bowl, leaving shells on. Pour oil into a blender. Add red pepper, garlic, and salt. Whirl until smooth. Pour over prawns. Marinate 1 hour or more, at room temperature, stirring once or twice. Thread shrimp on skewers. Grill over coals until shrimp turn pink.
Makes 4 servings

"O Uakh, I have come unto thee
I have eaten my food
I am master of choice pieces of the flesh of oxen
and of feathered fowl,
and the birds of Shu have been given to me"
The Papyrus of Ani
Translated by E. A. Wallis Budge

The delicate flesh of shellfish is best protected by grilling right in the shells. Each person gets his own skewer with lime wedges and a bowl of sauce Kerkennaise.

CREVETTES GRILLÉS À LA KERKENNAISE
The Famous Grilled Shrimp of Tunisia

3 pounds large shrimp in the shell
Olive oil
Salt and freshly ground pepper
Lime wedges

Sauce Kerkennaise
2 medium tomatoes, peeled and chopped
   (about 1-1/2 cups)
1/3 cup olive oil
1/4 cup chopped parsley
2 tablespoons minced green onion
1 clove garlic, crushed
1 teaspoon salt
1/2 teaspoon each crushed hot red pepper and
   freshly ground black pepper
1/4 teaspoon sugar

First prepare the sauce by mixing together all the ingredients; chill.
   Dip shrimp in olive oil, then season with salt and pepper. Thread shrimp on skewers and grill over coals until shrimp turn pink. Arrange shrimp, lime wedges, and a small pot of the Sauce Kerkennaise on individual serving dishes.
Makes 8 servings

The French influence is strong in Tunisia, since it was a protectorate from 1881 to 1956. But before that, Berbers, Arabs, Andalusians, and Turks contributed to a unique cuisine—including the fierce sauce called *berberé* in Ethiopia and *brisa* in Tunisia. Every house has its own way of preparing these sauces. It is said that you must eat your meat raw, for the sauce gives the impression of cooking the meat on your tongue.

BERBERÉ
The Red Pepper Paste of Africa

1 teaspoon ground ginger
1/2 teaspoon each ground cardamom and coriander and fenugreek seeds
A good pinch each ground cloves, cinnamon, and allspice
2 teaspoons minced onion
1 clove garlic, crushed
1 tablespoon salt
1/4 cup paprika
1 tablespoon crushed hot red pepper
1 teaspoon cracked peppercorns

Put all ingredients in a heavy skillet. Over low heat, toast 2 or 3 minutes, stirring. Cool. Put in a blender and whirl to pulverize. Use dry or make a paste with a little water and oil.
Makes approximately 3/4 cup

GRILLED CHICKEN BERBERÉ
With Niter Kebbeb

2 broiler chickens, halved
2 to 4 tablespoons Berberé, preceding
1/2 cup Niter Kebbeb, following

Rub both sides of chicken with Berberé (lightly, for less "fire"). Let stand at room temperature for about 2 hours. Grill chicken over coals, brushing frequently with Niter Kebbeb, until nicely browned, about 30 minutes.
Makes 4 servings

This clear butter oil of Ethiopia is softly seasoned with spices, and because it is clarified, it can be kept at room temperature for several weeks for brushing the flavor of the Orient over grilled kabobs, chicken, and fish.

NITER KEBBEB
Spiced Butter Oil of Ethiopia

2 pounds butter
1 small onion, chopped
4 cloves garlic, crushed
4 slices ginger root, mashed
1-1/2 teaspoons ground turmeric
1 cardamom pod, slightly crushed
1-inch piece cinnamon stick
4 whole cloves
1/2 teaspoon freshly grated nutmeg

In heavy saucepan over low heat, melt butter slowly. Add all remaining ingredients. Simmer, uncovered, 20 minutes. Strain through several layers of cheesecloth into a bowl, discarding seasonings. Store in covered jar in refrigerator.
Makes approximately 3 cups

This is the famous Moroccan "McDonald's," highly spiced and herby.

THE KEFTA OF MOROCCO *very good*

2 pounds very finely ground beef
2 teaspoons salt
1 teaspoon each crushed hot red pepper and
    coarsely ground black pepper
1/2 teaspoon ground cumin
1/3 cup each finely chopped fresh mint, parsley,
    and coriander
1 large onion, grated
Peanut oil

Mix together all ingredients, except oil, and let stand an hour or so to mellow flavors. Mold 3 egg-shaped balls on each skewer, brush with oil, and grill over coals until nicely browned, about 8 minutes in all. *–Do not over cook.*
Makes 4 servings

SLATA MESHWA
Tunisian Salad of Fresh Vegetables
Charred over the Coals

3 large green bell peppers
6 medium tomatoes
3 medium onions
1/4 cup olive oil
1 tablespoon white vinegar
2 cloves garlic, crushed
3 tablespoons capers (optional)
1/2 teaspoon crushed hot red pepper
Salt and coarsely ground black pepper to taste
1 hard-cooked egg, sliced
Lemon slices

Cut off tops of peppers; remove seeds and ribs, leaving peppers whole. Skewer peppers, tomatoes, and onions separately and grill over the coals until vegetables are charred on all sides, about 15 minutes. Remove from skewers and discard skins from peppers and tomatoes. Chop vegetables coarsely. Beat oil and vinegar until thickened. Stir in garlic, capers, red pepper, salt, black pepper, and vegetables; cover and refrigerate 1 hour before serving. Garnish with egg slices and lemon slices.
Makes 6 servings

The eighteenth-century traveling gastronome would scoff at the culinary activity in Africa, save those coastal regions visited by European and Near Eastern explorers, merchants, and slavers. Yet the Gods, the creators, like Mulunga, Leza, Nyambe, Mawu, Amma, were lavish with their seeding of the forests, jungles, and veldts with an astonishing array of wildlife, all suitable for the noble table. Monkey and roast locust were considered kingly delicacies. When ivory was poached, the elephant meat went to the villages for a feast. Strips of jerkied python, tasting like chicken, accompanied the hunting parties in their quest for wild beast, wild boar, crocodile, and the score of fishes in high mountain streams. Some claim with enthusiasm that a joint of ostrich, roasted over bright coals on the veldt will equal, no surpass, gigot d'agneau rôti.

In Tangier, beside the steep winding streets of the old town and the Casbah, the braziers are aflame with skewers of beef, lamb, and liver, with little squares of fat in between the pieces of meat. Everybody takes his unbaked bread to a central oven. When the bread is still warm from the baking, you tear off a goodly chunk, wrap it around the sizzling skewer, and slide the meat off.

THE QODBAN OF TANGIER
Kabobs Strung with Little Squares of Fat
Between the Pieces of Meat

2 pounds beef, lamb, or liver, cut into 1-1/2-inch squares (fillet may be used, but less expensive cuts are often more flavorsome)
Approximately 1/4 pound beef or lamb fat, cut into small squares
1 large onion, finely chopped
2 tablespoons minced parsley
2 teaspoons each salt and freshly ground pepper
2 teaspoons cumin seeds, crushed

Mix all ingredients together with your hands in order to incorporate the spices. Marinate at room temperature 2 hours. String meat on skewers, putting a small piece of fat between the pieces of meat. Grill over coals, turning to brown evenly, until done but still pink.
Makes 6 to 8 servings

The Portuguese led an entire continent into a new range of food. Angola reflects the Portuguese-Brazilian influence, and Mozambique, that of the Arabs, Indians, and Chinese.

ANGOLAN DUCK WITH GRILLED PAPAYA

5- to 5-1/2-pound duck, halved or quartered
1/4 cup corn oil
12 whole cloves
1 fresh hot chili pepper, chopped
1/2 cup fresh orange juice
2 tablespoons fresh lime juice
1/2 cup finely chopped green bell pepper
1/4 teaspoon salt

Grilled Papaya
2 firm papayas, peeled, halved, and seeded
4 tablespoons butter, melted
1/8 teaspoon freshly grated nutmeg
1/2 teaspoon salt

Place duck pieces in a shallow glass dish. Mix together all remaining ingredients and pour over duck. Marinate 2 hours at room temperature, turning occasionally. Grill duck over coals until nicely brown, about 10 minutes on each side.

Just before duck is cooked, prepare papayas. Put papayas in a bowl with melted butter, nutmeg, and salt. Turn to coat. Grill over coals until just heated through.
Makes 4 servings

In Algeria, the highpoint of the feast is a *mechoui,* a spitted whole baby lamb roasted over an open fire while the wizened turbaned Algerians sit cross-legged on patterned rugs looking on. The feast begins when the meat is tender enough to be stripped from the carcass with fingers. The *mechoui* also indicates lamb that has been grilled over braziers with a baste of butter and spices.

THE MECHOUI OF ALGIERS
**Grilled Lamb Chops
with Spiced Green Peppercorn Butter**

6 thick lamb chops
1 lime, cut in half
Salt and freshly ground pepper
2 teaspoons bottled green peppercorns, drained
1 small clove garlic
1/2 teaspoon ground cinnamon
4 tablespoons unsalted butter, softened
Imported kumquats, preserved in syrup

Rub chops with one of the lime halves and sprinkle with salt and pepper. Grill over coals until brown, but still pink inside. Meanwhile, crush peppercorns with garlic and cinnamon. Work in the butter until smooth. Squeeze a little lime juice from remaining half over each chop and top with some of the green pepper butter and kumquats with a little syrup.
Makes 6 servings

Hildadonga Duckitt, the Fannie Farmer of South Africa, explains in her book *Where Is It* that the word *sosatie* is derived from two Malay words—*sate* meaning "spiced sauce" and *sesate,* "skewered meat." Originally, the Malayans marinated their meat in fried onions, curry powder, chilies, garlic, and tamarind water.

SOSATIES OF SOUTH AFRICA
Lamb on Bamboo Skewers with a Curry Marinade

3 pounds lamb from leg, cut into 1-1/2-inch cubes
Salt and freshly ground pepper
3 medium onions, quartered
1 clove garlic, crushed
4 small dried hot red chili peppers
2 tablespoons brown sugar
2 tablespoons curry powder
2 bay leaves
1/4 cup fresh lemon juice
2 tablespoons chopped fresh coriander (optional)

Season lamb with salt and pepper. Toss with all remaining ingredients. Marinate 2 to 4 hours at room temperature, stirring occasionally. Thread on bamboo skewers and grill over coals, brushing with marinade and turning frequently, until nicely browned, about 8 minutes in all.
Makes 6 to 8 servings

NORTH ASIA

CHINA

Dungeness crabs will do for this recipe, but my favorite choice are those little blue shell crabs found squirming and snapping about at the Dupont Market on San Francisco's Grant Avenue. Accompany them with some simple dipping sauces to complement the fragrant crab meat.

GRILLED CRAB

6 live blue shell crabs

Dipping Sauce I   Peanut or olive oil, thinly sliced onion, and salt

Dipping Sauce II   Thin soy sauce and Oriental sesame oil

Dipping Sauce III   Thin soy sauce, finely grated ginger root, sugar, and fresh lemon juice

First prepare the dipping sauces. To prepare Dipping Sauce I, pour a few tablespoons peanut oil in a small bowl. Add the slivered onions and salt to taste, crushing the salt and onions into the oil with the back of a spoon. Taste and adjust with more onions and salt. To prepare Dipping Sauce II, simply float a little sesame oil atop a couple of tablespoons of soy sauce, adjusting amount to taste. To make Dipping Sauce III, combine soy sauce with all other ingredients to taste.

The crabs should first be washed (be careful of those snapping claws) and then dropped into boiling water for about 1-1/2 minutes. (You can forego this step if they are not too fiesty and you feel you can control them on the grill.) Place crabs on grill and cook, turning once, about 8 to 10 minutes; crab shell will turn pink when cooked. Remove from grill and let each guest crack their own. Serve with dipping sauces.

Makes 6 servings

Hoisin sauce, which is readily available in Oriental markets, is the mahogany-hued accompaniment to Peking duck as well as any number of Chinese dishes. I find it addictive, one of the best and most unusual of all basting sauces.

HOISIN SAUCE
TO BASTE CHICKEN, DUCK, SHRIMP, PORK

1/3 cup each soy sauce and rice vinegar
1/4 cup each brown sugar and white sugar
3 tablespoons hoisin sauce
1 clove garlic, crushed
2 tablespoons peanut oil
A good pinch of crushed hot red pepper

Mix all ingredients and use to baste grilled chicken, duck, shrimp, or pork.
Makes approximately 1-1/2 cups

The Chinese word for yam literally translates as "foreign potato," an acknowledgement of the fact that the Portuguese introduced this vegetable to China.

YAMS ON THE GRILL

First parboil yams (the small ones are the sweetest and best) for about 10 to 15 minutes, or until just barely cooked but still firm when pierced. Place them unwrapped, or wrapped in foil, on the grill. Heat over the coals just until soft and fragrant. Serve with warm, mild-flavored honey for dipping.

Kimun Lee, friend, amateur chef, and world traveler has contributed this Chinese treatment for an elegant bird. For those times when squab is too dear, try chicken wings or thighs in this soy sauce bath. Just as delicious.

KIMUN'S GRILLED SQUAB

2 whole squabs, about 1 pound each
1/3 to 1/2 cup thin soy sauce
4 cloves garlic, crushed
3 slices ginger root
1 tablespoon dry sherry
1/2 teaspoon sugar
Shredded lettuce

Combine all ingredients, except lettuce, coating squabs well. Let stand 1 to 2 hours at room temperature. Balance squabs on a spit and grill over coals about 20 minutes or until nicely browned, basting with marinade as they cook. Remove squabs from spit and cut into bite-sized pieces. Place on a platter on a bed of lettuce.
Makes 4 servings

Maggie Gin is my highly esteemed culinary comrade and author (with Alfred Castle) of the enlightening *Regional Cooking of China.* She is my mentor for this recipe for Peking duck, which is excellent roasted in your smoke oven or on a spit.

In San Francisco's Chinatown you can watch the process—sort of like blowing up a balloon. The duck's carcass is made airtight by tying up the neck opening and then the skin is inflated away from the flesh until it is tight. The duck is roasted slowly until the thick fat skin becomes crisp and golden. This skin is the real delicacy and is to be eaten with a piece of the flesh, a spring onion, and sweet hoisin sauce in a little sandwich of folded pancakes, which are as thin and white as paper doilies.

MAGGIE GIN'S PEKING DUCK SIMPLIFIED

4- to 5-pound Long Island duckling
2 teaspoons salt
1/2 cup honey or molasses
1 cup boiling water
1/4 cup soy sauce
Hoisin sauce or plum sauce
Chinese Pancakes, following
1 bunch green onions, cut into brushes*

Wash duck and remove excess fat. Bring a large pot of water to boil, and dip duck into boiling water for 2 minutes just to scald skin. Water will not return to boil. Remove duck from pot, pat dry, and rub cavity with salt. Hang duck in a shady, drafty place for 4 hours to dry. Combine honey with the boiling water. After the duck has been drying for 2 hours, brush the duck with honey mixture 3 or 4 times during remaining 2 hours to saturate the skin. This will crisp the skin while duck is roasting. Set bird breast side up on a greased grill of a covered barbecue. Place drip pan underneath. Cook duck about 2-1/4 hours, or until meat thermometer registers 170°F. Mix soy sauce with 2 tablespoons hoisin sauce and baste duck frequently with mixture during last 30 minutes of

roasting. Remove duck, slice off skin, and cut skin into pieces 1-1/2 inches by 2 inches. Slice meat into bite-sized pieces. (Reserve bones for soup stock.) Serve skin and duck pieces with hoisin sauce or plum sauce and pancakes. Garnish with onion brushes.
Makes 6 servings

*Using whites of onion only, cut into 2-inch lengths and then cut lengthwise into thin shreds up to 1/2 inch of end. Crisp in ice water.

CHINESE PANCAKES

Gradually add 3/4 cup boiling water to 2 cups unbleached flour, blending well with chopsticks. Turn dough out onto a floured board and knead for 3 to 5 minutes, or until dough is soft. Cover with dampened tea towel and let rest 30 minutes. Knead again for 1 minute and with hands roll dough into a 1-1/2-inch-thick rope. Cut into 16 equal pieces and flatten each piece to 1/2-inch thickness. Brush a little peanut oil or Oriental sesame oil on top of each round and press together with another oiled round, oiled sides touching. Roll out into a circle to fit a 6-inch crêpe pan. Heat an ungreased crêpe pan and cook rounds, one at a time, for 30 seconds per side. The pancake is ready to turn when golden spots appear on the underside. Immediately remove from heat, separate the joined rounds and stack on a plate. Cover until all rounds have been cooked.
Makes 16 pancakes

One of the favorite Chinese seasonings is *kuo pei* or dried tangerine peel, which gives a sweet tangy aromatic flavor to foods. The peel is used with poultry, pork, fish, and wild game. You can buy it in Chinese grocery stores, make it at home, or mix the homemade with the more pungent commercial product and store the two together in a jar. To make the peel, simply slice off the outer part or the zest, place it in a shallow pan, and cover it with cheesecloth. Set in the sun or in a turned-off oven and leave until well dried.

TEA-SMOKED DUCK WITH ANTIQUE TANGERINE PEEL

1 tablespoon each salt and crushed Szechwan peppercorns
1 Long Island duckling, about 4 pounds
1 teaspoon saltpeter
1/2 cup each rice and black tea leaves
2 tablespoons dried tangerine peel

Place salt and peppercorns in a dry skillet. Heat over a medium fire until peppercorns are pungent and salt is golden. Remove from fire and let cool.

Wash duck and pat dry. Rub inside and out with a mixture of the spiced salt and saltpeter. Hang duck in a shady, drafty place to dry for about 6 hours. Mix together rice, tea and tangerine peel and toss on hot coals in a smoke oven. Set duck in the oven and cook 2-1/4 hours, or until meat thermometer registers 170°F; add more tea and peel as needed for smoke. Cut into bite-sized pieces to serve.
Makes 4 servings

Here is another contribution from Maggie Gin.

CANTONESE-STYLE
BARBECUED SPARERIBS

3 pounds lean pork spareribs
1/4 cup each hoisin sauce and sugar
1 tablespoon rice wine or dry sherry
1 tablespoon Chinese oyster sauce
1/2 teaspoon five-spice powder
1/2 teaspoon saltpeter (optional; gives pork the
   red color)

Cut spareribs in half lengthwise and crack ends; keep in 2 pieces. Rub with a mixture of all remaining ingredients and marinate at least 4 hours at room temperature. Place on a grill high above the coals and cook, watching carefully that they do not burn and turning occasionally, about 45 minutes to 1 hour.
Makes 4 servings

Royalty of the Han era dined on epicurean delights, inspired by worldwide influences . . . roast suckling pig stuffed with dates, ribs of the fatted ox cooked tender and succulent, stewed turtle and roast kid, served up with yam sauce. Yet the "peasant meal" of those close to the earth or the sea was indigent to the environs. Bean curd soup, the bowl of rice, broiled pork, and fish.

Some of the more colorful sights in a Chinese community are the shops and restaurants selling barbecued meats. *Cha shu,* or barbecued pork, is one of the most popular of these meats and makes a delicious addition to stir-fried vegetables or noodle dishes. Here is how to make your own, which can then be frozen and kept on hand for use in spur-of-the-moment stir-fries.

CHA SHU
Chinese Barbecued Pork

3-pound boneless pork butt, fat removed
2 cloves garlic, crushed
1/3 cup each hoisin sauce and soy sauce
3 tablespoons each sugar and rice wine or
   dry sherry
1/2 teaspoon saltpeter (optional; gives pork the
   red color)

Cut the pork butt into strips about 1-1/2 inches square and 3/4 inch thick. Combine all remaining ingredients and marinate pork at room temperature for 3 or 4 hours. Place the strips on a grill raised high above the fire. Turn strips frequently until cooked through, basting with marinade. The pork should be cooked in about 30 to 40 minutes; test with a knife before removing from grill. To use, slice thinly. May be frozen up to 2 months.

For the Chinese, the sheep is the symbol of filial piety—the lamb respectfully kneels at its mother's side for milk. It is a meat that is mostly eaten in the north of China, especially by the Chinese Mohammedans who eschew pork as profane.

This spicy-hot lamb kabob is once again compliments of Kimun Lee.

BARBECUED LAMB

1-1/2 pounds lamb from leg, cut into 1-1/2-inch chunks
3 cloves garlic, crushed
2 green onions, sliced
1-1/2 tablespoons each thin soy sauce and hoisin sauce
3/4 teaspoon crushed hot red pepper
1-1/2 teaspoons dry sherry
1 teaspoon sugar
3 tablespoons chopped fresh coriander
1/2 teaspoon or more curry powder (optional)
Coriander sprigs

Combine all ingredients, except coriander sprigs, coating lamb well. Let stand at room temperature about 2 hours. Thread lamb on bamboo skewers and grill over coals, turning and basting with marinade, for about 8 minutes in all. Do not overcook; lamb should be pink and juicy. Set skewers on a platter and garnish with coriander sprigs.
Makes 4 servings

Chinese jerky has a different texture from "cowboy" jerky because it is cooked in two stages—the first cooking makes it easier to slice the meat thinly and helps keep the pieces from curling. The second cooking allows the meat to absorb the flavors.

CHINESE BEEF JERKY ON THE GRILL

3-pound sirloin tip
2 cups water
1/2 cup soy sauce
2 tablespoons red wine or dry sherry
1/4 cup sugar
1 teaspoon salt
2 whole star anise (or 5 whole allspice and 1 teaspoon anise seed)
1-inch piece ginger root, thinly sliced
3 small dried hot red chili peppers
Peanut oil

Trim fat from meat. Cut into strips about 3 inches thick and wide. Heat all remaining ingredients, except oil, in a large skillet. Add meat, cover, and simmer 20 to 30 minutes. Remove meat from liquid, reserving liquid, and chill meat until cool and firm. Cut meat in thin slices across grain. Bring soy mixture to a simmer and add meat slices. Cook, uncovered, until liquid is absorbed, about 40 minutes.

To cook over the coals, brush meat with a little oil and set on grill. Turn almost immediately or let char a little longer for drier jerky. Store in the refrigerator for up to 2 months.
Makes approximately 1 pound

JAPAN & KOREA

My favorite technique for cooking fish is the Japanese *shioyaki*, the simplest and purest way to preserve the freshness. Salting the fish before grilling causes the fat to break down, thus basting the flesh as it cooks. After grilling on one side and turning, the fish is done at precisely the point when the milky-white juices begin to flow.

SHIOYAKI
The Incomparable Method of Salt-broiling Fish

The best salt for fish is sea salt, available in the specialty section of many supermarkets or in health-food stores. To prepare a whole fish, dip the tail and fins into salt, then wrap them in foil to keep them from burning. Salt the rest of the fish lightly and let stand for 30 minutes. Grill the fish over coals. To cook them the Japanese way so that they appear to be swimming, insert a skewer through the fish at the point where the head meets the body, then out through the base of the tail.

The Japanese catch more fish than any other people in the world. The most important catch is *maguro*—fresh tuna. The *maguro* are laid out in rows on the wharves and tagged with the time and place where they were caught. Before grilling over the coals, the steaks are sprinkled with sea salt as in *shioyaki,* then rubbed with mint, garlic, and soy.

MAGURO
Fresh Tuna with Mint, Garlic, and Soy

4 tuna steaks, about 1 inch thick
Sea salt
2 large cloves garlic, minced or crushed
2 tablespoons soy sauce
2 to 3 tablespoons finely chopped fresh mint or
    coriander
Lemon wedges

Lightly salt steaks and let stand 30 minutes. Mix together garlic, soy, and mint. Rub over steaks and grill over coals quickly. Serve with lemon wedges. Makes 4 servings

Shintoism, the ancient religion of people who identify closely with land and sea, is important in the blessing and purifying of the fishing boats. That must be why the Japanese shellfish is extraordinary.

YAKI-HAMAGURI
Baked Clams with Salt Coating

12 clams in the shell
2 egg whites, lightly whisked
Sea salt
Rice wine (mirin) or dry sherry
Soy sauce
Pine needles

Scrub clams. With a sharp knife, carefully sever ligament between shell. Dip shell in egg white, then completely coat with salt. Grill over coals for about 5 minutes. Lift up the top shell of each clam and sprinkle the meat with a little rice wine and soy sauce and then close the shells. Avoid spilling any of the clam liquor. Arrange 3 or 4 clams on each serving dish, and sprinkle with a few pine needles. Serve immediately.
Makes 2 or 3 servings

KAKI NO REMON-SU
Grilled Oysters with Lemon-Radish Dressing

12 oysters in the shell
2 tablespoons grated Japanese radish (daikon)
1 teaspoon soy sauce
2 tablespoons rice vinegar or cider vinegar
2 tablespoons fresh lemon juice
1/2 teaspoon grated lemon zest
Minced fresh chives

Place oysters in a hinged grill and set over coals until they open, about 5 to 10 minutes. Combine the radish, soy sauce, rice vinegar, and lemon juice and zest. Pour the dressing over the oysters. Sprinkle lightly with minced chives, and serve at once.
Makes 2 or 3 servings

EBI ISOBE YAKI
Shrimp Grilled in a Wrapper of Seaweed

12 shrimp, shelled and deveined
1 tablespoon sake or dry sherry
1 tablespoon soy sauce
2 sheets nori (seaweed) or foil

Slash inner curve of shrimp to straighten. Marinate 1 hour at room temperature in mixture of sake and soy sauce. Drain off marinade. Wrap each shrimp snugly in a small piece of nori. Arrange on grill, seam side down, over coals. Broil until nori is glazed.
Makes 3 or 4 servings

One of the most fascinating fishermen is the cormorant, who has fished in Japanese waters for over 1200 years. Troutlike fish called *ayu* are lured by flames of burning pine boughs to where they are easy prey for these fish-catching birds on long leashes. The rings around the necks of the birds prevent them from gulping down their catch. The fish are sent off to the restaurant boats where they are grilled—preferably, this way for me.

AYU NO KOGAMI-YAKI
Trout Stuffed with Scrambled Eggs, Wrapped in Bacon

4 medium trout, dressed
Sea salt
2 eggs, lightly beaten
Freshly ground pepper
3 or 4 fresh mushrooms, finely chopped
6 snow peas, chopped
2 teaspoons butter
4 slices bacon

Wash trout and pat dry. Sprinkle with salt and let stand 30 minutes. Season eggs with a little salt and pepper and scramble very lightly with mushrooms and snow peas in butter. Stuff each trout with some of the egg mixture. Skewer closed. Wrap each trout with a slice of bacon, secured with a wooden pick. Place in a hinged grill and cook slowly over the coals, turning once, until fish flakes easily.
Makes 4 servings

The crevices of the reef at Tateyama have been filled with concrete, forming fish preserves that are stocked with crayfish. The crayfish, in turn, stock the restaurants, where they are skewered in their protective armor and grilled over charcoal.

ISE-EBI NO TERIYAKI
Crayfish Grilled with Soy and Rice Wine

2 pounds large crayfish or prawns in the shell
1 cup soy sauce
1/4 cup rice wine (mirin) or dry sherry
1/4 cup sugar
Lemon wedges

Wash the crayfish. Pull off the legs, but do not shell. Spear 3 crayfish on each bamboo skewer. Combine soy sauce, rice wine, and sugar in a large pan and heat until simmering on the edge of the grill. Grill crayfish on both sides about 10 minutes in all, brushing with sauce several times as they cook. Dip crayfish in sauce just before serving. Serve with lemon wedges.
Makes 6 servings

From the sizzling charcoal fires of the food wagons come *yakitori* of chicken, chicken livers, and scallions cut like little brushes. Tiny quail eggs, gingko nuts, shellfish, and vegetables are skewered, too.

YAKITORI

Marinade
1/4 cup sake or dry sherry
2 tablespoons soy sauce
2 teaspoons sugar

Basting Sauce
1/2 cup rice wine (mirin) or dry sherry
1/2 cup soy sauce
2 tablespoons sugar
2 whole chicken breasts, halved, skinned, boned
   and cut into cubes
1-1/2 pounds chicken livers
1 green bell pepper, cut into squares
6 green onions, trimmed to 3 inches and
   slashed at the ends
Japanese seasoned pepper (sansho) or
   cayenne pepper

Mix marinade ingredients and pour over cubed chicken and livers. Mix basting ingredients in a small saucepan and bring to a boil on edge of grill. Drain two-thirds of the livers and string on skewers with green pepper. String chicken cubes and remaining livers on skewers with green onions. Set on grill over coals and cook quickly, basting often, about 3 minutes on each side. Serve with seasoned pepper.
Makes 8 servings

Matsusaka beef is considered the finest in Japan. Little wonder, for the animals are pampered to death. They are stall-fed, given beer to drink to stimulate their appetite, and massaged daily to distribute their fat evenly. The texture of the beef is evenly fat and lean, "salt and pepper" in Japanese.

GYUNIKU NO AMI-YAKI
Grilled, Marinated Beef

1 tablespoon rice wine (mirin)
1 tablespoon Oriental sesame oil
1 tablespoon sugar
2 tablespoons toasted sesame seeds
2 cloves garlic, crushed
2 tablespoons finely chopped green onion
1-1/2 pounds club steaks, sliced 1/4-inch thick
Soy sauce
2 tablespoons grated ginger root
Dash of cayenne pepper

In a shallow platter combine rice wine, sesame oil, sugar, sesame seeds, garlic, onion, and 2 tablespoons soy sauce. Add the beef, toss well, and let stand 20 minutes. For the dipping sauce, mix ginger, cayenne pepper and 1/2 cup soy sauce. Pour into individual dishes. Grill the beef quickly over coals, a few slices at a time. Serve with the sauce.
Makes 4 servings

Is there a more auspicious time for an elegant teppan-yaki-style feast with the fresh bounty of both sea and soil than when brothers meet again? One of the honored samurai, and the host, a gentleman well versed in the calligraphic arts. The classical greeting of the swords is as old as the Empire itself.

The cooking of Japan is very elemental—that is, it swings with the elements and the seasons more than any other cuisine. The first gastronomic event of autumn hails the appearance of the *matsutake,* a mushroom as big as a steak, which is picked and cooked over charcoal on the spot.

GYUNIKU TERIYAKI
Japanese Fillet and Dried Mushrooms

4-pound whole beef fillet
4 ounces large dried forest mushrooms
1 cup hot water
1/2 pound butter
1 pound fresh mushrooms, thickly sliced
6 green onions, diced
2 cloves garlic, crushed
Salt and freshly ground pepper
Sugar
1/4 cup brandy, warmed in a small pan placed
    on the grill

Have your butcher tie the fillet with a thin layer of fat. For the sauce, soak the forest mushrooms in the hot water 5 minutes; drain. Heat the butter until it sizzles and add the dried mushrooms, fresh mushrooms, green onions, and garlic. Cook until vegetables are tender. Season with salt, pepper, and sugar to taste. Flame with brandy.

In a smoke oven with a drip pan, roast fillet 20 to 30 minutes, or until meat thermometer registers 130°F for rare, brushing with sauce frequently. Slice fillet and pass the remaining sauce.
Makes 6 to 8 servings

The salt-broiling method of cooking fish works with chicken as well, breaking down the fat under the skin to keep the flesh moist. *Teriyaki* translates as "shining broil," and the marinade does double duty, even triple duty, as a marinade, basting sauce, and dipping sauce.

TORI TERIYAKI
Fresh Lemon Chicken

1 fat broiler chicken, quartered
Sea salt
2 lemons
1-inch piece ginger root, peeled and sliced
2 tablespoons soy sauce
2 tablespoons rice wine (mirin)
1 tablespoon Oriental sesame oil
1/4 cup peanut oil
4 cloves garlic, crushed
Chopped fresh coriander

Wash chicken and pat dry. Sprinkle with salt and let stand 30 minutes. Grate the zest and squeeze the juice of 1 lemon into a bowl with the rest of the ingredients; reserve the other lemon. Marinate chicken in mixture at room temperature 2 hours or more, turning occasionally. Grill chicken about 20 minutes or until nicely browned, brushing with marinade. Arrange chicken in serving dish. Pour rest of marinade over all. Thinly slice reserved lemon. Garnish chicken with lemon slices and coriander.
Makes 4 servings

From Marianne Maruyama, one-time resident of Yokohama and now of San Francisco, a recipe for little eggplant slices spread with a sauce sweet like candy with an edge of saltiness—the result of that ever-present Japanese ingredient, miso.

GRILLED EGGPLANT

1 pound Japanese eggplants, or
1 medium globular eggplant
2 tablespoons each white and red miso (soybean paste)
2 to 3 tablespoons honey
2 to 3 tablespoons sesame seeds, toasted in a dry pan until they pop, then ground with a mortar and pestle

Cut Japanese eggplants into 1/2-inch-thick slices; if using globular eggplant, first cut it in half lengthwise and then in 1/2-inch slices. Grill eggplant over coals until browned and very soft. While eggplant is cooking, prepare the sauce by combining the two misos in a small pan placed on the side of the grill; the miso will soften as it heats. Add honey until the sauce is very sweet. Stir in sesame seeds. Spread the sauce thickly on the eggplant slices and serve. Makes 3 or 4 servings

At Hahn's Hibachi, a Korean barbecue house in San Francisco, the menu is divided into four sections—the *buhl-goghi* or barbecue dishes, the *jung-gol* or broth dishes, the raw meat and fish dishes called *whai,* and the side dishes like *kimchee,* a spicy, hot relish that complements the marinated meat. This Korean method of cutting through the ribs allows the marinade to penetrate and cuts down on the cooking time.

SOOJA KIM'S KOREAN CRISSCROSS RIBS

4 pounds lean beef short ribs
1/4 cup each soy sauce, dry red wine, and brown sugar
1 bunch green onions, chopped
2 cloves garlic, chopped
1-inch piece ginger root, sliced
1/4 cup peanut oil
2 tablespoons toasted sesame seeds

Have your butcher cut the short ribs about 3 inches square. At home, place the ribs bone side down. Make diagonal cuts through meat halfway to the bone; then make cuts the opposite way, forming X's. Mix together all remaining ingredients in a shallow dish and marinate ribs, cut side down, 2 hours or more at room temperature. Grill ribs over coals, basting with marinade, about 30 minutes, or until nicely browned but still pink inside.
Makes 4 servings

SOUTH ASIA & THE PACIFIC

INDIA & PAKISTAN

The genius of Hindu cooking lies in the intricate mixtures of ground and whole spices, mild or strong, "wet" or dry, as in the *garam masalas* of aromatic spices.

GARAM MASALA
Ground Spice Mixture

1 cup cardamom pods (yields 1/3 cup seeds)
5 cinnamon sticks, each about 3 inches long
1/4 cup whole cloves
1/2 cup cumin seeds
1/4 cup coriander seeds
1/3 cup peppercorns

Shell cardamom seeds, discarding pods. Spread all spices on a jelly roll pan. Place in a preheated 200° oven for about 25 minutes, stirring occasionally. Crush cinnamon sticks with mallet or rolling pin then whirl all toasted spices in blender, 1/4 cup at a time, until pulverized, stopping as needed to stir. Store in covered container at room temperature.
Makes approximately 1-3/4 cups

Ghee is real butter, very carefully clarified so that it won't become rancid over a lengthy period of time. But in India where milk and butter are luxuries, the "real thing" has its substitutes in vegetable oils. Local oils are used very often—coconut oil in Karala, mustard oil in Bengal, peanut and sesame oils in various parts of northern India—and each gives a distinctive flavor to the cooking.

GHEE
Indian Butter Oil

Heat 1 pound butter in heavy pan over moderate heat. Increase heat and bring to boil. When it foams, stir; then reduce heat to lowest setting. Simmer uncovered 20 minutes. Milk solids on bottom will look golden under the transparent butter layer. Strain through a fine sieve lined with several layers of damp cheesecloth. Repeat process if any solids pass through. Store in covered container in the refrigerator. Keeps 2 months or more.

Indian cooking requires an intuitive feel for spices, since they vary from place to place and time to time. This chicken dish is considered a true test of intuition.

MURG MASALAM
Whole Chicken with Masala

2 fryer chickens, halved

Masala
1 large onion, sliced
3 tablespoons ghee, page 143
2 cloves garlic
2-inch piece ginger root, peeled and chopped
2 small dried hot chili peppers, seeded
2-inch cinnamon stick, crushed
6 whole cloves
1 tablespoon each poppy seeds and cumin seeds
1 tablespoon salt
1/4 to 1/2 cup water

To prepare the masala, sauté onion in ghee until lightly golden. Put into blender with remaining masala ingredients. Whirl smooth at high speed. Make a few slits in meaty parts of chickens. Press masala into them. Rub all surfaces with masala. Marinate for 1 hour at room temperature. Grill chicken over coals, turning and basting frequently, about 35 minutes, or until cooked through.
Makes 4 servings

For no definable reason, the food of a country always tastes better if you eat the way the natives do—in India, with your fingers. Once you know how, you will believe the story about the Shah of Iran in India, who supposedly remarked that to eat with a fork and spoon was like making love through an interpreter. You must always eat with your right hand and always allow yourself to be served. Your right hand would leave the serving spoon sticky and you must not touch it with your left.

MURG KABAB
Pakistani Chicken "Heart and Soul"

1-1/2 pounds chicken breasts, halved, skinned, boned, and cut into large cubes
1/2 pound chicken hearts
1/2 pound chicken livers
2 cups plain yogurt
Grated zest and juice of 1 lemon
1 onion, chopped
2 cloves garlic, crushed
2 teaspoons grated ginger root
A good pinch of each ground cinnamon, cloves, and cumin, and salt and freshly ground pepper

Thread chicken breast meat onto bamboo skewers alternately with hearts and livers. Arrange skewers in a single layer in a shallow dish. Mix together rest of ingredients for marinade; adjust seasonings. Pour over chicken, cover, and marinate at room temperature 1 hour or so. Grill over coals until nicely browned, about 8 to 10 minutes.
Makes 6 servings

The traditional accompaniments to the tandoori dishes are green onions, white radish, fresh lime wedges, and brine pickles.

TANDOORI GRILL
A Mixed Grill of Chicken, Shrimp, and Lamb

18 large shrimp in the shell
3 broiler chickens, halved (or 6 chicken legs and thighs joined)
2 pounds boneless lamb from the leg, cut into 1-1/2-inch cubes

Marinade
1/2 teaspoon saffron threads
3 tablespoons boiling water
1/2 cup fresh lime or lemon juice
1 tablespoon salt
1/4 cup garam masala, page 143
6 small dried hot chili peppers, crushed
1 large onion, quartered
2 garlic cloves, crushed
1-inch piece ginger root
1 cup plain yogurt
1/2 teaspoon red food coloring

Combine all ingredients for marinade. Snip the shrimp shells, but leave them on. Marinate shrimp in enough of the marinade to moisten. Make several 1/2-inch-deep cuts in the chicken and brush generously with marinade. Combine lamb cubes with enough marinade to coat well. Marinate meats and shrimp overnight in the refrigerator.

Thread shrimp and lamb cubes on separate skewers. Place chicken on grill over coals and cook, basting with marinade, about 40 minutes. About 10 minutes before chicken is cooked, put lamb on grill and, basting and turning frequently, cook until nicely browned. Just before meats are cooked, place shrimp on the grill and cook until they turn pink, 3 to 4 minutes.
Makes 6 servings

In northern India where lamb is king of the beasts, an inventive cook could present a superb lamb dish for every day of the year. A good example is this kabob of lamb steaks or round bone chops marinated in a pungent yogurt that also serves as a sauce.

LELA KA KABAB
Marinated Lamb Chops with Pungent Yogurt

8 thick-cut lamb chops or steaks
2 onions, quartered
1 cup coriander sprigs
1-1/2 teaspoons salt
1 teaspoon each ground cloves, cardamom, ginger, and cinnamon, and poppy seeds and freshly ground pepper
2 tablespoons ghee, page 143, or butter
2 cups plain yogurt
1/3 cup fresh lemon juice

Arrange meat in a shallow dish. Put all remaining ingredients in a blender and whirl until smooth. Rub mixture on meat. Marinate several hours or overnight in the refrigerator. Grill lamb quickly over coals and serve with remaining marinade as a sauce.
Makes 8 servings

Vishnu, as the primeval cosmic man (in Maya) extends over earth, oceans, and space . . . . Whilst Lord Rama, successful in the quest for Sita, enjoys a light repast.

RAAN
Delhi Spiced Lamb

6- to 8-pound leg of lamb, butterflied
2 onions, chopped
3-inch piece ginger root, peeled
6 cloves garlic, crushed
3/4 cup fresh lemon juice
1 tablespoon ground coriander
1 teaspoon each ground cumin and turmeric
2 teaspoons garam masala, page 143
1/2 cup peanut oil
Coarse salt and pepper
1 teaspoon orange food coloring, Spanish bijol,
    or Indian food coloring
Radish flowers and onion rings, crisped in ice water

Make small slashes with a sharp knife on both sides of meat. In a blender, purée onion, ginger, and garlic with the lemon juice. Add spices, seasoning and food coloring, blending well. Rub marinade well into the slashes and over surface, or fold up meat in a bowl with marinade. Let stand in the refrigerator at least 24 hours, turning frequently. Pat meat dry. Grill over coals about 20 minutes on each side, basting with marinade, until meat thermometer registers 135°F for medium rare, or to your taste. Garnish with radish flowers and onion rings. Slice lamb on the diagonal to serve.
Makes 10 to 12 servings

The early Sanskrit writings dating from about 1200 B.C. make it quite clear that meat was commonly eaten at that time and that the fatted calf was a special luxury for ceremonial feasts. Today the slaughter of cattle is outlawed for the Hindus—but doubly deprived are the Kashmiri Brahmins, who are forbidden onions and garlic because they are suspect of heating the blood and unleashing passion.

KASHMIRI KABOB
Ground Lamb with a Gingery Snap

2 pounds lean ground lamb
2 teaspoons salt
1 teaspoon freshly ground pepper
1/4 cup chopped fresh coriander
1/2 teaspoon each ground cumin and garam
    masala, page 143
Pinch of powdered saffron
1/4 cup chickpea flour
1/4 cup finely ground almonds
1 tablespoon finely chopped ginger root
Juice of 1 lemon
2 tablespoons plain yogurt

In a large bowl combine lamb and all remaining ingredients, blending well. Shape mixture into 18 cylinders, 2 inches long, on waxed paper-covered plate. Chill. Thread meat onto skewers and grill quickly over coals, about 4 minutes on each side. Arrange kabobs on plates. Sprinkle with additional garam masala.
Makes 6 servings

Your Pakistani picnic might include these spicy grilled meatballs stuffed with almonds, served with a curry sauce and condiments on *chapatis*—the marvelous bread that balloons on the grill.

KOFTA KARI
Ground Beef Meatballs, Stuffed with Almonds

24 blanched almonds
2 pounds lean ground beef
1 large onion, finely chopped
1/2 cup chopped fresh coriander
1/8 teaspoon powdered saffron
1-inch piece ginger root, finely chopped
1 egg
6 tablespoons chickpea flour
2 tablespoons garam masala, page 143
Dash of cayenne pepper
Curry Sauce, following

In saucepan, cover almonds with water. Bring to boil, remove from heat, let cool and drain; set aside. Put meat in a bowl and with fingertips, mix in remaining ingredients. Shape 24 meatballs, pushing an almond into the center of each. Broil over hot coals, in well-oiled, hinged grill, until brown. Provide hot Curry Sauce to spoon over meatballs. Makes 6 to 8 servings

CHAPATIS
Bread That Balloons on the Grill

2 cups atta (fine whole wheat flour)
1 teaspoon salt
2/3 cup water
4 tablespoons ghee, page 143

In a bowl, mix the flour, salt, and water. Knead mixture until it holds together. On a floured board, knead about 3 minutes. Wrap in plastic and set aside for 30 minutes. Divide into 14 balls. Roll each ball out on a floured board into a 5-inch circle, rolling on both sides evenly. Stack floured circles between sandwich bags; seal in a plastic bag and chill until ready to use.

Set grill about 4 inches from coals. Place chapatis on dry grill. As blisters pop up around edges, press firmly toward center with a spatula. When fully puffed and lightly browned, turn over and bake about 2 minutes more. Brush with ghee. Makes 14 chapatis

CURRY SAUCE

1 large onion, chopped
2 cloves garlic, mashed
3 tablespoons ghee, page 143
1 teaspoon each ground turmeric and cumin
2 medium tomatoes, peeled and chopped
1 teaspoon salt
1/2 cup plain yogurt

Sauté the onion and garlic in ghee until translucent. Add turmeric, cumin, tomatoes, and salt. Bring to a boil, reduce heat, and simmer 5 minutes. Stir in the yogurt and keep warm until serving. Makes approximately 1-1/2 cups

SOUTHEAST ASIA

Bali was described by Nehru as "the morning of the world" and it is here that the spice flavors are the most vivid, the tastes clear and defined, the ceremonial foods at their most picturesque. A favorite combination of spices called *bumbu megenep* —chilies, ginger, garlic, onion, bay, and sesame seeds with a couple of pungent native roots—makes for a happy rainbow of flavors in every dish Balinese.

SATE LILEH BUMBU
The Long Fish Sticks of Bali

6 firm-fleshed fish steaks, cut into long strips
2 teaspoons crushed hot red pepper
1-inch piece ginger root, peeled
1 large onion, grated
2 cloves garlic, crushed
A good pinch each ground turmeric, sesame
   seeds, salt and freshly ground pepper
1/4 cup peanut oil

Marinate strips of fish in mixture of all remaining ingredients at room temperature 1 hour or so. Thread on bamboo skewers and brush with more oil. Cook over coals, brushing with marinade, until nicely charred but still moist, about 8 to 10 minutes in all.
Makes 6 servings

For each of the 10,000 temples in Bali there is an *odalan,* a birthday celebration commemorating the date of the temple's consecration. A carnival spirit prevails, with games, contests, barkers selling wonder tonics, and the inevitable food stalls or *warongs,* many run by young girls in pursuit of husbands. The food is a feast—plates of fried rice beribboned with chilies, cool tropical salads and drinks, spicy meat cakes cooked over the coals on skewers, fragrant coconut cakes, and the thick coffee of the island.

THE SPICY MINCED MEAT OF BALI

1 pound each coarsely ground pork and beef
2 cloves garlic, crushed
2 teaspoons ground coriander
1 teaspoon freshly grated nutmeg
1/2 cup chopped green onions
1 egg, lightly beaten
Salt and freshly ground pepper
Peanut oil

Mix together all ingredients except oil and shape into 8 patties. Place patties in hinged grill and set over coals. Brush with oil and cook until nicely charred.
Makes 8 servings

By day, Orchard Road Car Park is just that. By night, it is a maze of mini-restaurants offering the whole spectrum of Malaysian food, cooked over charcoal and butane fires, many with giant woks atop the grills. Not so facetiously dubbed "Glutton Square," you hardly know where to start—or stop —in selecting your evening meal. Perhaps some *poh pia,* Singapore-style egg roll, a selection of *satay,* the crispy tidbits of charcoal-grilled meats, fish, and chicken on bamboo skewers. Or, perhaps, a "steamboat," the Malay version of fondue, with bubbling broth to cook the skewers of delicacies.

"GLUTTON SQUARE" SATAY
The Unofficial National Dish of Malaysia, Singapore, and Indonesia

4 pounds boneless chicken, meat and/or fish, cut
    into 1-inch cubes
2 tablespoons curry powder
1/2 cup each peanut oil and soy sauce
4 cloves garlic, crushed
2 tablespoons brown sugar

Marinate meats in a mixture of all remaining ingredients for 4 hours or overnight in the refrigerator, keeping different kinds separate. Thread meats on bamboo skewers, leaving about 1 inch between pieces, and grill over coals until nicely charred on all sides. Serve with Kuak Satay, Ketupat, and Mentemun Dan Bowang, following.
Makes 6 to 8 servings

KETUPAT
Pressed Rice Cubes

1-1/2 cups short-grain pearl rice
2-1/2 cups water
Salad greens

In a saucepan combine rice with water. Bring to a boil uncovered over high heat. When water disappears from surface of rice, lower heat, cover, and simmer 25 minutes or until water is absorbed. Press firmly and evenly into a 9-inch square pan. Cover and chill. Run a knife around the edge of the pan and turn rice out onto a board. Cut in squares about the size of the satay meat. Serve at room temperature in a bowl lined with greens.
Makes 6 to 8 servings

MENTEMUN DAN BOWANG
Marinated Cucumber Salad

3 medium cucumbers
2 small red onions
1/4 cup each sugar and white wine vinegar
1/2 teaspoon salt

Cut cucumbers in half lengthwise, then into crosswise slices about 1/2 inch thick. Do the same with the onions. Marinate cucumbers and onions in rest of ingredients. Cover and chill 2 hours.
Makes 6 to 8 servings

KUAK SATAY
Peanut Sauce

1 large onion, cut in chunks
2 cloves garlic
4 or 5 small dried hot chili peppers
1/4 cup peanut oil
2 teaspoons ground coriander
1 teaspoon ground cumin
1 cup roasted peanuts, finely ground
1-1/2 cups coconut milk, page 161
3 tablespoons brown sugar
2 tablespoons each fresh lemon juice and soy sauce

Purée onion, garlic, and chilies in a blender. Heat oil in a small pan and add purée, coriander, and cumin. Cook over medium heat 3 to 4 minutes. Reduce heat and stir in peanuts; then gradually stir in coconut milk, sugar, lemon juice, and soy sauce. Simmer gently until sauce thickens.
Makes approximately 2-1/2 cups

BEEF SATE WITH
PUNGENT PEANUT BUTTER

3 pounds top round steak, cut into 1-inch cubes
1/4 cup chopped fresh coriander
2 teaspoons each anise seed, cumin seed, salt,
   and sugar
1-inch piece ginger root, grated
1/3 cup each fresh lemon juice and peanut oil
A good pinch of crushed hot red pepper

Toss meat with all remaining ingredients and marinate, covered, 8 hours or overnight in the refrigerator. Thread meat on bamboo skewers, leaving about 1 inch between pieces, and grill over coals, basting with marinade and turning often, until nicely charred, about 6 to 8 minutes in all. Serve with Pungent Peanut Butter, following.
Makes 8 to 10 servings

PUNGENT PEANUT BUTTER

2 tablespoons peanut oil
1 small onion, chopped
3 cloves garlic, crushed
1 teaspoon each anise seed and ground cumin
1 or 2 small dried hot chili peppers
1 cup chunk-style peanut butter
1/4 cup fresh lemon juice
Coconut milk, page 161
Chopped fresh coriander

Combine oil, onion, garlic, anise seed, cumin, and chilies in a small saucepan placed on the side of the grill. Blend in the peanut butter, lemon juice, and enough coconut milk to make a saucy consistency. Top with coriander.
Makes approximately 2 cups

TJOLO-TJOLO
Broiled Fish and Vegetables with Three Sauces

3-pound whole dressed fish
Salt and freshly ground pepper
Melted butter
Tomato and Red Chili Sauce, following
Ketjap Sauce, following
Almond and Coconut Milk Sauce, following
Vegetables for garnish, such as tomatoes, carrots,
    cucumber, celery, etc.
Coriander sprigs

Season fish with salt and pepper and place in hinged grill. Grill over coals, brushing frequently with butter. Fish is done when it flakes easily with a fork, about 15 minutes to a side. Have the 3 sauces ready in small bowls. Cut vegetables paper thin and arrange attractively on a platter with the fish and sprigs of coriander.
Makes 4 to 6 servings

TOMATO AND RED CHILI SAUCE

2 tomatoes, peeled and chopped
2 fresh hot red chili peppers, seeded, if desired,
    and finely chopped
Juice of 2 limes
Salt and freshly ground pepper to taste

Combine all ingredients, mixing thoroughly. Adjust seasonings and let stand to allow flavors to blend.
Makes approximately 1 cup

KETJAP SAUCE

1/2 cup each water, brown sugar, and soy sauce
2 tablespoons molasses
2 slices ginger root
Dash each ground coriander and freshly ground
    pepper

In a saucepan combine the water, brown sugar, and soy sauce, stirring until well blended. Add the molasses, ginger root, and spices and bring mixture to a boil. Cook, stirring, 5 minutes. Remove from heat and let cool.
Makes approximately 1 cup

ALMOND AND COCONUT MILK SAUCE

1 cup each toasted blanched almonds and water
1 large onion, chopped
1 clove garlic, chopped
2 tablespoons peanut oil
1 teaspoon trassi (shrimp paste)
1 small fresh hot chili pepper, seeded, if desired,
    and chopped
1/4 teaspoon powdered sereh (lemon grass)
1/2 cup coconut milk, page 161
2 tablespoons tamarind liquid or fresh lemon juice
Salt and freshly ground pepper

Put almonds in blender with water. Purée on high speed. Sauté onion and garlic in oil until lightly golden. Blend in remaining ingredients and puréed nuts. Simmer 5 minutes. Taste for seasoning.
Makes approximately 1-1/2 cups

The food the Filipinos love has a cool, sour taste as opposed to the fiery-hot booby traps of many of the Asian dishes. The charcoal-grilled meats and chicken are often seasoned at the table with vinegar spiked with chili and pungent garlic and a *sambal* of chilies and onions.

RELLENONG MANOK
Philippine Roasted Chicken with Ham and Egg Stuffing

1 roasting chicken
Juice of 1/2 lemon
Salt and freshly ground pepper
1/2 pound boiled ham
3 all-beef frankfurters
1-1/2 pounds pork butt
1 large onion, cut up
1/4 cup raisins
2 raw eggs
1 teaspoon salt
3 small gherkins, chopped
2 large pimientos, chopped
2 hard-cooked eggs

Rub chicken, inside and out, with lemon juice, salt, and pepper. Let stand 30 minutes. To make stuffing, cut ham, frankfurters, pork, and onion into chunks and grind in meat grinder or food processor. Combine with all remaining ingredients, except hard-cooked eggs, mixing well. Stuff cavity of bird, putting hard-cooked eggs in center of stuffing. Truss openings. Set bird in a smoke oven and cook about 1-1/2 hours, or until juices run clear when thigh of bird is pierced. Serve with Philippine Garlic Sauce and Sambal Iris, following.
Makes 6 servings

PHILIPPINE GARLIC SAUCE

4 cloves garlic
1 teaspoon salt
1 teaspoon crushed hot red pepper
3/4 cup white wine vinegar

Mash garlic well and put in bowl with salt, pepper, and vinegar. Mix well. Store in covered jar in the refrigerator.
Makes approximately 1 cup

SAMBAL IRIS (NORTHERN SULAWESI)
Chili, Onion, and Lime Juice Condiment

1 medium tomato, diced
2 small fresh hot chili peppers, finely chopped (red or green)
1 medium onion, thinly sliced
Grated zest of 1 lime
Juice of 3 limes

Combine all ingredients in bowl and let stand 1 hour to allow flavors to blend before serving.
Makes approximately 1-1/2 cups

The Thailand curries differ sharply from others in their magical blending of pungent spices with the mellow flavors and fragrance of leaves. These *kaeng* curries are color coded—bright red, jungle green, turmeric yellow—each a particular blend of spices and herbs. In Bangkok, you could be served these curries in grand European manner at the famed old Oriental Hotel or, late in the evening, you could feast on them at the colorful Pratunam Market where they brighten the food vendors' stalls.

THAI CURRY PASTE

7 dried hot red chili peppers, seeded
2 green onions or shallots, coarsely chopped
2 cloves garlic, chopped
1 tablespoon trassi (shrimp paste)
1 tablespoon powdered sereh (lemon grass)
1 tablespoon ground laos (java root from the
   ginger family)
1 tablespoon paprika
1 teaspoon salt
1 teaspoon each coriander seeds and caraway seeds
Grated zest of 1/2 lemon

In blender, whirl all ingredients until puréed, scraping down sides as necessary. Store in covered jar in refrigerator.
Makes approximately 1/2 cup

Note For a green sauce, substitute green chilies for red ones and omit paprika.

MU OP
Siamese Roast Pork with Curry Paste and Pineapple

4-pound pork loin
1/4 cup Thai Curry Paste, preceding
Salt and freshly ground pepper
1 large pineapple
Chopped fresh coriander

Basting Sauce
1/4 cup soy sauce
1/4 cup white vinegar
6 tablespoons brown sugar

Puncture the pork in several places with a skewer. Rub the curry paste over the surface of the meat and into the puncture holes. Season with salt and pepper. Cut away the pineapple rind in one piece and tie rind around the top part of the roast. Balance roast on a spit or set in a smoke oven and cook for 1 hour. Remove pineapple rind and discard. Combine ingredients for basting sauce and baste meat heavily during the next 20 minutes of cooking, or until meat thermometer registers 170°F. Serve with fresh pineapple sections tossed with some of the basting sauce and some chopped coriander.
Makes 6 servings

AUSTRALIA & NEW ZEALAND

The Aussie's have developed a unique method of skewering food so it won't slip or fall off when you turn it over the fire. A large two-pronged skewer is threaded with jumbo "hairpins" that serve as individual skewers. That's the way they do their famous "carpetbagger" steaks, plump with succulent oysters.

CARPETBAGGER STEAKS
Aussie Filet Mignon Stuffed with Oysters

6 *filets mignons,* 2 inches thick
12 fresh oysters
Salt and freshly ground pepper
Peanut oil
Chopped parsley

Carefully cut a pocket in the side of each steak. Season oysters with salt and pepper and insert 2 in the pocket of each steak. Skewer opening. Season steaks with salt and pepper, then rub with oil. Grill over coals to desired doneness. Garnish with parsley and serve at once.
Makes 6 servings

One man's goose is another man's lamb, especially in New Zealand where it is likely to be on the daily bill of fare and the only culinary fuss is in the roasting over an open fire.

COLONIAL GOOSE
Smoked Leg of Lamb with a Bread Stuffing

5-pound leg of lamb, boned
Salt and freshly ground pepper
1 medium onion, chopped
2 tablespoons butter
3 cups fresh bread crumbs
1 egg yolk, lightly beaten
Handful of chopped parsley
Pinch of chopped fresh thyme

Season all sides of lamb with salt and pepper. Set aside. Sauté onion in butter until translucent. Stir in bread crumbs and cook 3 minutes more. Take off heat and add remaining ingredients, adjusting seasonings to taste. Let cool. Put stuffing into cavity of lamb. Skewer closed securely, or tie with string. Balance meat on a spit or set in a smoke oven and cook 1-1/2 to 2 hours, or until thermometer reaches 135° to 145°F for medium rare.
Makes 8 servings

THE PACIFIC

When the Portuguese and Spanish explored the Orient, the ubiquitous "nut of India" got a new name. Since the three black spots at the end of the shell look like the comic face of a clown, or *coco* in Spanish, the *coconut* was launched from there to Timbuktu. The Pacific Islander drinks coconut water, gets drunk on its blossom toddy, eats the meat and drinks the milk, wears coconut clothes, lives in a coconut-thatched house, burns husks and shells for fuel, makes music, sweeps the floor, and paves his way with this miraculous nut.

HOW TO MILK A COCONUT

Crack open the coconut and pour off the liquid. Peel off the brown skin from the coconut meat and break the meat into small pieces. Put the meat in a blender with enough hot water to make a thick purée, and blend, stopping the motor as necessary to clean the sides of the container. Turn into a strainer lined with 2 thicknesses of damp cheesecloth. Squeeze out liquid and discard pulp.

For coconut top milk or "cream," let milk stand in the refrigerator until liquid separates and then skim off the top part. Coconut milk will keep, refrigerated, for 4 to 5 days. One cup chopped coconut meat plus 1 cup water yields about 1 cup coconut milk.

Note Coconut milk may also be made by using unsweetened dessicated coconut in the same manner as the fresh coconut meat. The milk may also be purchased canned and frozen in specialty food markets and some supermarkets.

LIME-MARINATED SCALLOPS WITH COCONUT SAUCE

1 pound scallops
Salt and freshly ground pepper
Melted butter
Lime wedges

Dipping Sauce
1/2 cup sour cream
1 cup coconut top milk, preceding
2 green onions, finely chopped

Thread scallops on bamboo skewers. Season with salt and pepper and brush with butter. Combine all ingredients for dipping sauce, blending well. Grill scallops quickly over coals, a minute on each side. Serve with sauce for dipping and garnish with lime wedges.
Makes 4 to 6 appetizer servings

"Ua mau ke ea o ka 'ainaika pono . . ."
Going to the Hukelau.

The ancient Hawaiians, like most people, believed that the best and proper way to honor their gods was by the feast. And the modern Hawaiians believe that the best and proper way to honor anything and everything is by the feast, specifically the *luau.* The word pertains to the leaf of the taro plant, the root of which is pounded into *poi,* and also pertains to the dishes cooked in leaves, so you'll be served *luau* at the *luau* along with the traditional Kalua pig and numerous other Asiatic delights.

The old Polynesian taboos have changed, but the male tradition is perpetuated in the preparation of the pig and the other dishes that go into the *imu,* or pit, where the *luau* is cooked. On some of the islands, indeed, it is all a matter of high protocol, with rank and seniority determining the cut of pork to which each guest is entitled.

KALUA PIG
Or, How to Dig an *Imu* and Toss Your Own *Luau*

If you like big, fat pigs the way the Hawaiians do, you must dig a pit accordingly. Smaller pigs weighing about 25 pounds are easier to handle and not so greasy. Dig your pit about 4 feet long by 4 feet deep by 4 feet wide. Stick a sturdy pole right in the center of the pit. This is important as it serves as a little "chimney" in which you will light your fire. Lay kindling and wood on the bottom of the pit, a good foot of it, then 60 or so round, smooth lava stones that can stand extreme heat without bursting. (You'll need another couple of dozen stones to put into the pig's stomach, so heat them in the *imu* at the same time.) When you're ready to light the fire, pull out the pole. Wrap a cloth around a long broom handle and dip it into fire lighter, ignite it, and poke it into the hole.

Meanwhile, your pig should be cleaned, scraped, and drawn. Make little slits in the skin, taking care not to cut into the meat. Rub coarse salt into the slits and into the cavity. Fill the stomach with heated stones and tie the legs together.

Lay several banana trunks across the width of the pit. (This is one of the fine points of the craft and with practice, you will be able to precisely adjust the temperature of the oven by adjusting the thickness of your stalks.) Wrap your pig in a heavy chicken wire basket lined with ti and banana leaves, and surround with yams, bananas, fish, and meat, all tied up in banana leaf packages. Cover with a thick blanket of leaves, a dozen or so burlap bags, and then a final covering of earth or sand. Let the food steam for 4 or 5 hours. The Hawaiians like their pig cooked to a fare-thee-well, so cut down on the time, if you prefer.
Makes approximately 16 servings

When you go to Hawaii, your introduction to the culinary blend of cultures might well be the *pupu*, the snacks the islanders love in profusion: pork, chicken, fish, and tropical fruit grilled over the coals, cherry tomatoes stuffed with oysters and salmon, canned litchis with gingery cream cheese, coconut chips, fried wonton for dipping into a bath of soy, Chinese dumplings called *dim sum*, Portuguese sausage, American hot dogs.

CHO CHO
**Broiled Skewered Steak with
Sweet and Sour Sauce**

Flank steak (1 pound or more)
1 cup soy sauce
3/4 cup brown sugar
2-inch piece ginger root, finely grated
1 tablespoon Chinese oyster sauce
2 tablespoons sake

Put meat in freezer for a short time to make slicing easier, then slice diagonally, 1/8 inch thick. Thread on bamboo skewers, looping slices back and forth. Mix remaining ingredients in saucepan and set on side of grill to heat. Brush meat with sauce. Grill quickly over coals, basting, until crisply browned, about 2 to 3 minutes.
Makes approximately 36 skewers

A Tahitian specialty is chicken pressed into a section of green bamboo, which is closed at one end by the joint and stuffed with ti leaves at the other end. These are put into the *ahimaa,* or pit, with the pig. But you can also cook them right in the coals if you can lay your hands on some bamboo—and serve the dish right in the bamboo bowls with a ti leaf wrapper.

TAHITIAN CHICKEN BAMBOO

1 onion, chopped
2 cloves garlic, minced
4 tablespoons butter
1 tablespoon curry powder
6 whole chicken breasts, halved, skinned, boned,
    and diced
1/2 pound fresh mushrooms, sliced
2 tablespoons chopped fresh coriander
Salt and freshly ground pepper
Coconut top milk, page 161
Ti leaves

Sauté onion and garlic in butter until translucent. Add curry powder and cook, stirring, 3 minutes. Then add chicken and mushrooms and cook until chicken is tender. Add coriander and season with salt and pepper. Add just enough coconut milk to bind and lightly flavor the mixture. Adjust seasonings. Spoon mixture into clean, hollow bamboo sections, each with a closed joint. Stuff top with ti leaves and toss into the coals to heat.
Makes 6 servings

SMOKE COOKING

COOKING WITH SMOKE

This special section on smoke cooking deals in detail with the method of smoking at low, even temperatures. However, you can give a smoky flavor to any of your barbecues by simply adding chunks or chips of aromatic woods or cuttings to your coals. This might be called smoke roasting or grilling, as opposed to smoke cooking, which gives a richer smoke. And cold smoking is a different process altogether—although the ancient Chinese "beehive" in which the meat hangs in a chimney well away from the coals combines the two methods.

You can, of course, smoke-cook in any covered barbecue, from an elaborate unit to a simple hibachi with an up-ended kettle for a lid, but the cooking times and results will vary. It's best to follow your own manufacturer's directions for specifics.

Once you have learned the basic principles of smoke cooking, you can adapt many of the other recipes in this book to that method.

SMOKE COOKING

Smoke, salt, and sun are the ancient ingredients for preserving food. But since we're no longer dependent on this method for preserving, we can use those simple principles to develop the subtleties of smoke cooking. Cold smoking, which is more of a curing process, is not covered in this book.

There is no end to the types of smokers you can use, ranging from the popular cylindrical smoke-cookers to innovative oil drums, old refrigerators, and Rube Goldberg contraptions. You need a heat source and a smoke source. I prefer water smokers, which have a water pan positioned under the grill. This keeps the flesh moist and succulent however long the smoke. The recipes in this section are all designed to be used with water smokers.

Once you know the quirks of your own smoker and have learned how best to keep the temperature low and steady, you have it made, for the actual cooking is practically fuss-free. The specially designed smoke-cookers that allow you to smoke at low even temperatures give somewhat different results than does your covered barbecue, and in any case there are a lot of variables. It's important to follow your own manufacturer's directions with any piece of equipment.

THE HEAT

First build a charcoal fire in the fire pan. Most smokers are open at the bottom for air and covered

*Mist sounds soft on the azure tiles
while a Hon-Maguro smokes in the* damada . . . .
Maneki-Neko guards yet bids welcome.

at the top to hold in heat and smoke with optimum control. (Charcoal briquettes are the most common heat source, but some smokers have an electric element and some are convertible.) *The single most important factor in smoke cooking is keeping the temperature low and that means in the 170° to 225° range.* Some smokers have built-in thermometers that make it easy to keep track of the temperature, but they are not always accurate. You can double check by keeping an oven thermometer on the grill.

Keep a pan of briquettes burning down in a separate fireproof container so you can add a few as needed along with soaked wood chips. (If you are using an electric smoker, check the manufacturer's directions to see whether you need to soak the wood.)

THE WATER PAN

Cold-smoking dries and preserves food. Water smoking keeps it moist and flavorsome.

Most of the new smokers have a fire pan at the bottom, a water pan in the center, and a grill on top. Any smoker can be converted into a water-smoker: a disposable foil pan or an old roasting pan works very well as a water pan. Mound your coals around the water pan or on one side with the food directly above the water pan to catch the juices and prevent the fire from flaring up. Just as you can vary your smokes, you can vary your water—with a fruity wine, a pungent vinegar, herbs, or citrus peels. Or you can marinate your food, then pour the marinade into the water pan. As the water evaporates, the juices become concentrated.

You can mop them up with thick slices of bread or use them as natural sauces for whatever you're smoking. When you hear a sizzling sound you know it's time to add water. You can pour it right through the grill without removing anything.

THE SMOKE

Start soaking wood chunks, chips, or aromatic twigs 15 or 20 minutes before your fire is ready. This keeps them from burning when you add them to the fire pan and allows them to smolder slowly. You will need 4 to 6 chunks of wood or 1 quart of chips for larger roasts and turkeys and about half that for smaller items. However, because there are many variables in smoke cooking, and because smoke escapes every time you raise the lid, you should always keep extra chips soaking in case you need them.

Mesquite, hickory, and oak chunks and chips are available commercially. You can use any kind of fruit wood, walnut, aspen, or alder. Note: Wood from pine, cedar, or other evergreen trees contains pitch and resins and should be avoided. Throughout the book are suggestions for using various aromatics that add to the excitement of your smoked foods.

THE FOOD

There is almost nothing that you can't smoke, even a batch of hard-cooked eggs. These are the most important points to remember:

• You must always refrigerate your smoke-cooked foods unless you eat them right away. Don't count on keeping them any longer than you would non-smoked foods unless you freeze them.

• Allow yourself plenty of time. All sorts of variables affect smoke-cooking times: the type of charcoal, the temperature, the wind, and the altitude.

• Buy yourself two good thermometers: one to check the temperature of the smoker, the other to take an instant reading of the food. (See the smoke cooking charts in this section for times and temperatures for cooking specific foods.)

• One of the real advantages of smoke cooking is that foods keep moist and juicy in the smoker for an hour or two after they are done.

• Another advantage is that the smoke flavor becomes richer after a day or two in the refrigerator. You can smoke-cook ahead of time.

• Be sure to keep the water pan full. That's the secret of this kind of cooking. For large roasts and turkeys, you'll probably have to add water a couple of times.

• For a long smoke, you'll need to keep charcoal briquettes burning down in a separate pan so you can add them to the fire pan as necessary. Keep some wood chips or chunks soaking in water to replenish the smoke.

• Resist the temptation to smoke-cook a whole meal. The few vegetables that take well to smoke cooking might be better the next day in a smoky ratatouille or in a hearty peasant soup.

• You can cut down on your smoke-cooking time by partially cooking foods in the oven before smoking, or by finishing them off in the oven after you have sufficient smoke flavor.

• Every time you peek into the smoker you allow both heat and smoke to escape. Add 15 minutes to the cooking time for each peek.

ELECTRIC SMOKERS

Since there are many types of electric smokers, it's important to follow your own manufacturer's directions and cooking charts. Some electric smokers require a 110V AC outlet and others a 120V AC outlet. Some require any wood chips to be soaked while others specify dry flakes; some electric smokers don't use wood. In any case, when you are smoke cooking with added wood, you should keep your smoker outside in a well-ventilated area. And you can count on such timing variables as wind, rain, outside temperature, and altitude. As in smoke cooking with charcoal, allow yourself some leeway in timing and you won't have anything to worry about.

ELECTRIC AND GAS BARBECUES

There are certain advantages to electric and gas barbecues in that you don't have to fuss with the fire and ashes. Since they require only a brief preheating, there's no waiting around for the coals to die down, but as a general rule the cooking time is about the same as in charcoal cooking if you keep an even temperature.

Outdoor units that use bottled gas can be moved around on their wheels. Units that use natural gas are generally connected to a permanent gas line, and electric units need only to be plugged into an outlet. Some of these barbecues come with lava rock or other material in the shape of briquettes. When the sizzling juices hit the rocks, the ensuing smoke gives the "barbecue" flavor.

As is true with all equipment, it's best to read your own manufacturer's directions carefully. And, most important, use a good thermometer to take your own readings rather than relying on a table.

COMBINATION COOKING

There are times when it is desirable to use a combination of cooking techniques to cut cooking time or to achieve a more delicate smoke flavor. The trick is to smoke-cook at very low heat (between 150° and 170°F.) in your covered barbecue or smoker until the meat or poultry is golden brown, generally between 3 and 4½ hours. You can finish it off in the oven at 325°F. or let cool, wrap in plastic or foil, and refrigerate for up to 3 days. Finish cooking in the oven, using your thermometer to check doneness. For longer storage, you can freeze the partially cooked food, thawing it before finishing it off in the oven. In this section you will find combination techniques that call for steaming or braising before smoke cooking.

DRY CURES AND BRINES

Since smoke cooking is not a preserving process, the subtleties of flavor and texture of the food are important. Although you don't have to dry-cure or brine your fish, meat, poultry, or game, these treatments definitely add to the appearance and flavor of the finished product. Brining gives a better appearance, but drying the food before cooking it takes much longer than with a dry cure. For a dry cure, sea salt or coarse (kosher) salt, which has no added magnesium carbonate, is mixed with sugar, herbs, and spices. In either case, the food to be smoked has to be rinsed thoroughly

and air-dried, so you can count on it taking some time. The approximate times for dry curing and brining are given in the chart on page 165.

ABOUT MARINADES

Marinades are used to flavor and tenderize meats. In contrast to brining and dry curing, which are salt processes, the time required for marinating foods is much briefer. The recommended times are 1 to 3 hours at room temperature, and "overnight" or up to 30 hours in the refrigerator. Throughout this book you'll find marinades for all types of dishes (see "Sauces, Marinades, and Condiments" in the index).

A BASIC DRY CURE
For Meats, Fish, and Poultry

1 cup sea salt or coarse (kosher) salt
1/4 cup brown sugar, firmly packed
Herbs and spices (optional)

Mix salt and sugar, adding your own favorite herbs and spices. Use as much cure as you need and store the rest in an airtight container. Rub over surfaces of meat, fish, or poultry and into the cavities. Wrap the food in a plastic bag and refrigerate. (See curing times in chart on page 165.) After food is cured, rinse the cure thoroughly from surfaces and cavities under cold running water. Pat dry with paper towels. Air-dry for 2 hours until surface is glossy (you can hasten the process by placing the food in front of a fan). Then proceed with the smoke-cooking directions for that kind of food.

A BASIC BRINE

3-1/2 quarts water
1-1/2 pounds sea or coarse (kosher) salt
1 pound dark brown sugar
Mixed seasonings (bay leaf, thyme, garlic,
  juniper berries, peppercorns, cloves,
  allspice, mace)

Fill a large pot with the water, salt, and sugar. Tie your own selection of herbs and spices in a square of cheesecloth and toss into the pot. Bring to a boil over medium heat; simmer, stirring occasionally, 5 minutes. Cool. Discard spice bag. With a butcher's needle or clean ice pick poke several 1/2-inch holes in meat to allow brine to penetrate. Place meat in a well-scrubbed deep non-metallic crock (porcelain, stoneware, glazed earthenware, or glass). Cover with brine, adding water, if necessary. Weight meat with a non-metallic object such as a water-filled preserving jar or stack of heavy plates. Make sure meat is completely submerged before covering. Refrigerate.

Brining times vary with the thickness of meat, but since this is a flavoring rather than a preserving process, there are no hard and fast rules. Over-salting can be corrected by soaking meat in cold water. Never brine or cure different meats or poultry together. Always start with a fresh batch of brine. The range of time for brining is given in the chart to the right.

CURING AND BRINING TIMES UNDER REFRIGERATION

MEAT
Roasts, 3-4 lb.: up to 9 days
Roasts, 5-10 lb.: up to 12 days
Roasts, pork, 3-8 lb.: up to 12 days
Butterflied leg of lamb, 5-7 lb.: up to 9 days
Shoulder of lamb, 5-7 lb.: up to 9 days
Chops, lamb, 6-9 lb.: 4-10 hr.
Chops, pork, 6-12 lb.: 4-10 hr.
Ribs, pork, 5 lb.: 4-10 hr.
Ham, fresh, 10 lb.: up to 12 days
Sweetbreads: 4-10 hr.
Calves liver: 4-10 hr.

POULTRY
Chicken (cup-up or split), 1-4 lb.: 4-10 hr.
Chicken (whole), 2-2-1/2 lb.: 4-10 hr.
Chicken (whole), over 5 lb.: 6-24 hr.
Cornish hens and small birds, 1-3 lb.: 1-3 hr.
Duck, 3-5 lb.: 4-10 hr.
Goose, 8-10 lb.: 4-10 hr.
Pheasant, 3-5 lb.: 4-10 hr.
Turkey, 8-12 lb.: 12-24 hr.
Turkey, 13-18 lb.: 12-36 hr.

FISH
Whole small: 1-4 hr.
Whole large, 3-6 lb.: 6-10 hr.
Fillets: 30 min.-2 hr.
Steaks, 1 inch thick: 2-4 hr.
Shellfish: 30 min.-1 hr.

SMOKE-COOKING CHART FOR FISH
Smoker Temperature for Fish: 150°-170°F.

TYPE OF FISH	WEIGHT IN LB.	HOURS TO SMOKE: CHARCOAL	HOURS TO SMOKE: ELECTRIC
Whole: small		1-3	1 - 2-1/2
Whole: large	3-6	3-4	2-1/2 - 3-1/2
Fillets		1/2 - 2-1/2	
Steaks	1 inch	1/2 - 3	1/2 - 2-1/2
Shellfish		1/2 - 2	1/2 - 2

SMOKE COOKING FISH

1. Give a whole cleaned fish or large fillet A Basic Dry Cure, page 164, or A Basic Brine treatment, page 165, or use a marinade. Cover and refrigerate overnight. Small fish require only a few hours, and steaks and fillets do well with a simple marinade.

2. Rinse fish under cold running water, rinsing cavity thoroughly.

3. Air dry (put in front of fan to hasten process) until skin is glossy.

4. Make diagonal slashes about 2 inches apart on both sides of fish. Insert springs of herbs, strips of salt pork, or other seasoning deep into slashes.

5. Light briquettes in fire pan, varying the amount with the size of the fish.

6. Soak 1 to 3 wood chunks or 1/2 to 1 quart wood chips in water for 20 to 30 minutes.

7. When briquettes have burned to a gray ash, toss on the wood and other aromatics.

8. *It is most important in smoke cooking fish to keep the temperature low: 150° to 170°F.*

9. Put water pan in place and fill with water, marinade, or wine and herbs in various combinations.

10. Check temperature before setting fish on non-stick or oiled grill. If too hot, remove a few coals and wait until temperature drops.

11. Brush fish with oil or melted butter. Cover and smoke-cook 30 minutes to 4 hours until fish is opaque when flaked. *Take care not to overcook.*

12. Remove from grill and brush with vegetable oil or melted butter. Serve warm or cool and wrap in plastic to allow the smoke to settle in.

Far from the Playa, sunset washes orange at the quays of Old Palma, while the fishermen repair their nets for next morning's sail.

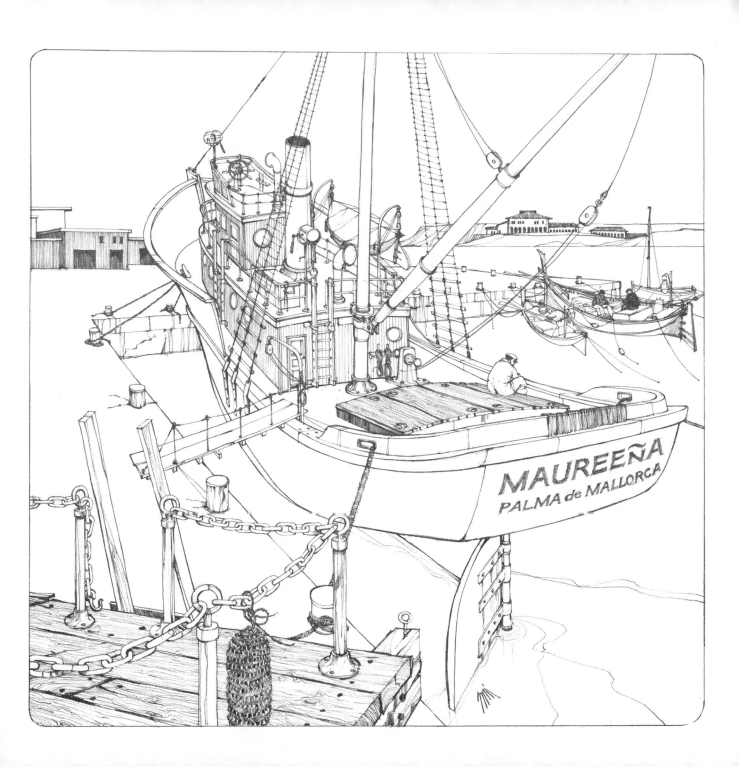

Parboiled fresh green leaves protect the skin and flesh of fish while basting it naturally with their own juices.

A BIG FISH SMOKED IN LEAVES
(Grape, Lettuce, Spinach, or Chard)

4- to 6-pound whole fish
A Basic Dry Cure, page 164 or
  A Basic Brine, page 165
3 to 4 heads of lettuce (or 30 to 40 grape or
  spinach leaves, or 2 bunches chard)
1 lemon, sliced thin
1/2 cup chopped mixed fresh herbs
Corn or safflower oil

Follow directions for treating the fish with basic cure or brine. The next day, rinse thoroughly and air dry until skin is glossy. Parboil leaves in a pot of boiling water about 3 minutes; drain. Line cavity of fish with lemon slices and herbs. Overlap leaves around fish from head to tail. Set water pan in place and fill with any combination of wine, water, and herbs. Check temperature to make sure it registers between 150° to 170°F. Set fish on grill. Cover and smoke-cook according to directions on page 166 until fish is opaque when flaked with a fork. Take care not to overcook. Remove leaves and lemon slices and discard. Brush fish with oil. Serve warm, or let cool, cover with plastic wrap, and refrigerate.
Makes 4 to 6 servings

Water pan: 3/4 full
Fire pan: 3/4 full
Smoke-cooking time: 3 to 4 hours
Electric smoker: 2-1/2 to 3-1/2 hours

When the tribal leader of the Skagit Indians came to San Francisco with his smoked salmon, jaded palates took note. This salmon was *different*. Not something you'd pile on a bagel, more like poached salmon. It was moist and delicate with a rich smoky edge, the glossy mahogany surface a surprising contrast to the intense salmon-colored interior.

PACIFIC INDIAN SALMON

3-pound salmon fillet with skin
A Basic Cure, page 164
1/4 cup corn or safflower oil
1/4 cup brown sugar
Bay leaves

Give the salmon the basic cure. Air dry until the skin is glossy, then rub surfaces with oil and brown sugar. Add a bay leaf or two to water pan. Smoke skin side down at very low temperature according to directions on page 166 until flesh is opaque when tested with a fork. To serve, slice diagonally into 1-inch pieces and accompany with a good sharp mustard and lemon wedges.
Makes 6 servings

Water pan: 3/4 full
Fire pan: 3/4 full
Smoke-cooking time: 2 to 3 hours
Electric smoker: 1-1/2 to 2-1/2 hours

A friend who was born and raised in Seattle described a whole salmon-trout stuffed from head to tail with tiny Olympic oysters and buttered cracker crumbs. For small fish, this simple vegetable stuffing seems just right. Or simpler yet, tuck a slice of bacon inside each fish.

SMALL WHOLE FISH

6 fresh fish, 1 to 2 pounds each
A Basic Dry Cure, page 164, or
 A Basic Brine, page 165
1/4 cup butter
2 cups chopped mixed raw vegetables
 (fennel, celery, green onions, leeks)
Minced fresh herbs
Salt and freshly ground pepper
Juice of 1/2 lemon

Give the fish the basic dry cure or brine treatment for 4 hours or so. Rinse thoroughly. Air dry until skins are glossy. In a skillet, melt butter and quickly sauté vegetables and herbs. Season the mixture with salt, pepper, and lemon juice. Spread about 1/3 cup of the filling into the cavity of each fish. Truss or skewer opening. Follow directions for smoke cooking fish, page 166, making sure your temperature is between 150° and 170°F. Set fish on non-stick or oiled grill, cover, and smoke-cook until flesh is opaque when flaked with a fork. Serve warm, or let cool, wrap in plastic, and refrigerate.

Water pan: 2/3 full
Fire pan: 1/2 full
Smoke-cooking time: 1 to 3 hours
Electric smoker: 45 minutes to 2 hours

DILLED LIME DRESSING
FOR SMOKED FISH

1/3 cup fresh lime juice
2 teaspoons grated lime zest
1 egg
2 teaspoons Dijon-style mustard
1-1/2 teaspoons dillweed
1 teaspoon sugar
3/4 teaspoon salt
Dash white pepper
1 cup corn or safflower oil
1-1/2 tablespoons chopped drained capers

Measure all ingredients except oil and capers into container of an electric blender. Add 1/4 cup of the oil. Blend 10 seconds. With motor running add remaining oil in a slow steady stream. Blend 30 seconds, scraping sides of container as needed. Stir in capers. Cover and chill.
Makes about 1-3/4 cups

FISH STEAKS AND FILLETS

In a glass bowl, coat fish steaks or fillets with marinade. Let stand at room temperature 2 to 3 hours, turning frequently, or up to 6 hours. Follow directions for smoke cooking fish, page 166, allowing 30 minutes to 3 hours for smoking. Make sure your temperature is between 150° and 170°F. Brush with marinade when you check the smoke and when you remove from grill. Serve warm, or let cool, wrap in plastic, and refrigerate.

Here are two marinades for big, fat fish steaks and 2-finger-thick fillets.

A SIMPLE TERIYAKI SAUCE

1 cup light soy sauce
2/3 cup medium-dry sherry
1/3 cup corn or safflower oil
1 tablespoon grated fresh ginger
2 cloves garlic, crushed

In a small saucepan heat ingredients to boiling. Cool. Marinate fish, covered, in refrigerator for 2 hours or more, turning occasionally.

A MARINADE WITH WINE AND HERBS

1 cup dry white wine
1/4 cup fresh lemon juice
1/4 cup corn or safflower oil
2 tablespoons mixed chopped fresh or
  crumbled dried herbs
Salt and freshly ground pepper

Bring the wine to a boil in a small saucepan. Cool. Add rest of ingredients and use to marinate fish, turning occasionally.

Most of us are purists when it comes to shellfish. However, a light smoke is nice for a change, and the shells serve as protective armor for the delicate flesh.

SMOKE-COOKED LOBSTER, CRAB, AND SHRIMP

Clean shellfish. Crack shells lightly to allow smoke to penetrate. Follow directions for smoke cooking fish, page 160, adding wine and herbs to the water pan. Check temperature to make sure it is between 150° and 170°F. Set lobster or crab on grill. Arrange shrimp in their shells on a foil tray. Smoke-cook 30 minutes to 1 hour until flesh is opaque. Take care not to overcook.

HOT GARLIC AND FRESH GINGER BATH

To finish off shellfish the Chinese way, arrange smoked shellfish on a tray or serving platter. Heat 1/4 cup corn or safflower oil in a small saucepan with 2 cloves garlic, crushed, and 1 tablespoon grated fresh ginger. Pour over shellfish and serve warm.

Off-season at the Cape, but soon the sea will yield its bounty.

SHELLFISH IN FRESH GINGER MARINADE

2 to 4 pounds shrimp in shells,
  cracked crab, or lobster
1/2 cup each corn or safflower oil, soy sauce,
  and dry sherry
1/4 cup chopped fresh ginger
1/4 cup fresh lemon juice
1 tablespoon sugar
1 cup sliced green onions

In a glass bowl or other non-metallic container, marinate shellfish in mixture of oil, soy, sherry, ginger, lemon juice, sugar, and green onions, turning frequently. Follow directions for smoke cooking fish, page 166, using marinade with added water in water pan. Take care not to oversmoke.
Makes 4 to 6 servings

These stuffed clams make a tasty appetizer or dinner for two when you have something else in your smoker. Take care that they don't burn if the temperature is high.

SMOKED STUFFED CLAMS CARIB

12 large fresh clams
4 tablespoons unsalted butter
1 medium onion, chopped fine
A good pinch dried thyme and
  crushed hot red pepper
1 cup finely diced French bread
6 tablespoons light cream or half and half
Grated Parmesan cheese
Chopped fresh parsley

Scrub clams. Bring 1 quart water to a boil. Add clams, reduce heat and simmer, covered, for about 6 minutes until shells open. Cool. Pour off juices into a bowl. Chop clams coarsely and set aside. Melt butter in a skillet. Sauté onions with thyme and red pepper for about 3 minutes. Add diced bread and continue cooking, stirring another 3 minutes. Remove from heat and add enough reserved clam juice to moisten. Correct seasoning. Fill as many shells as you need with the clam mixture. Spoon a little light cream over the clams and sprinkle with cheese. Set on a foil tray and put in smoker for 30 minutes. Sprinkle with parsley.
Makes 4 appetizer servings

SMOKE-COOKING CHART FOR POULTRY
Smoker Temperature for Poultry: 200°-225°F.

TYPE OF POULTRY	WEIGHT IN LB.	HOURS TO SMOKE: CHARCOAL	HOURS TO SMOKE: ELECTRIC	TEMPERATURE WHEN COOKED
Chicken: cut up or split	1-4	4-5	4-5	160°F.
Chicken: whole	2 - 2-1/2	5-6	5-6	160°F.
Chicken: whole	5	6-7	30-45 min. per lb.	160°F.
Turkey	8-12	7-8	4-5	160°F.
Turkey	13-18	10-12	5-6	160°F.
Cornish hens, small birds	1-3	3-5	3-5	160°F.
Duck	3-5	5-6	5-6	145°-160°F.
Goose	8-10	5-6	30-45 min. per lb.	160°F.
Pheasant	3-5	5-6	30-45 min. per lb.	160°F.

SMOKE COOKING POULTRY

1. Marinate the bird in a marinade or A Basic Brine, page 164, or rub with A Basic Dry Cure, page 165. Cover and refrigerate overnight.

2. Remove bird from marinade (reserve marinade) or follow directions if using basic dry cure or brine. In either case, air dry until skin is glossy.

3. Lean birds should be larded or covered with strips of fatback or bacon before smoke cooking.

4. Pour charcoal briquettes into fire pan and ignite.

5. Soak 1 to 4 chunks of wood or 1/2 to 1 quart of wood chips in water for about 20 minutes.

6. When coals are completely covered with gray ash (about 30 minutes), drain the wood on paper towels and add to coals.

7. Set water pan in place. Fill with reserved marinade and enough water to fill pan, or use any combination of wine and water, vinegar, herbs, etc.

8. Spray grill with non-stick coating or rub with vegetable oil and set in place.

9. Center bird on grill over water pan. Brush with marinade or vegetable oil. (Plug in electric smoker.)

10. Make sure temperature stays between 200° and 225°F. Add hot coals to increase temperature or remove one or two to decrease it. Add wood to maintain a steady stream of smoke.

11. Each time you check the bird, blot the surface with a paper towel and brush with marinade or vegetable oil.

12. Continue smoking until desired doneness. Serve warm or cool to room temperature. To store, wrap airtight and refrigerate.

A MUSTARD-HERB MARINADE
FOR CHICKEN OR VEAL

1/2 cup mustard (a combination of
  mustards is best)
2 tablespoons mustard seeds, crushed
2 tablespoons corn or safflower oil
1/4 cup dry white wine
1/4 cup chopped fresh herbs
  (or 2 tablespoons each crumbled dried tarragon,
  summer savory, sage, and thyme)

Mix mustard with rest of ingredients in a glass
bowl. Add chicken and roll to coat well. Marinate
several hours. Pat chicken dry with paper towels.
Use marinade to baste chicken during final half
hour of smoking.

PETALUMA'S PRIZE SMOKED CHICKEN

6-pound roasting chicken or capon
1 tablespoon grated lemon zest
1/2 cup fresh lemon juice
2 cloves garlic, crushed
2 tablespoons chopped fresh mint
1 tablespoon chopped fresh tarragon
1/4 cup corn or safflower oil

Truss chicken. Mix rest of ingredients in a large
glass bowl and add chicken. Marinate several hours
or overnight in refrigerator, turning several times.
Remove from bowl. Reserve marinade. Pat dry
with paper towels. Air dry (set in front of fan to
hasten process) until skin is glossy. Follow directions for smoke cooking on page 173. Brush
chicken with reserved marinade before, during, and
after smoking. Serve warm, or let cool, wrap in
plastic bag, and refrigerate.
Makes 4 to 6 servings

Water pan: 3/4 full
Fire pan: 3/4 full
Smoke-cooking time: 6 to 7 hours
Electric smoker: 30 to 45 minutes per pound

The tandoor ovens in the best Indian restaurants produce incomparable, brightly colored roasted birds.

TANDOOR-STYLE SMOKED CHICKEN

4 halved frying chickens, skins removed
1 tablespoon coarse (kosher) salt
2 cloves garlic, crushed
1/2 lemon
1 cup plain yogurt
1 teaspoon each cumin seed, ground coriander,
  cayenne pepper, coarsely ground black pepper,
  and red vegetable coloring
Melted butter, for basting

With a sharp knife, make small deep slashes all over chicken. Rub with salt, garlic, and lemon half. In a large glass bowl mix yogurt and seasonings for the marinade. Coat each chicken half, poking yogurt mixture deep into slashes. Pile chicken halves on top of each other in a non-metallic container, cover, and refrigerate 4 hours or overnight. Drain, reserving marinade. Brush with melted butter. Smoke-cook according to directions on page 173, basting when you lift cover to check the smoke, and when the birds are finished cooking. Serve hot, or let cool, wrap in plastic, and refrigerate.
Makes 4 servings

Water pan: 3/4 full
Fire pan: 3/4 full
Smoke-cooking time: 4 to 5 hours
Electric smoker: 4 to 5 hours

The best game birds I've been served have been in hole-in-the-wall restaurants like the little *tascas* of Portugal, where you can slather the richly smoked birds with a fiery hot sauce served in ceramic jugs and called *piri-piri*.

GLAZED SMOKE-COOKED GAME BIRDS

1 large lemon, halved
6 small game birds (Cornish game hens,
  guinea hens, squab, dove, quail)
Corn or safflower oil
Salt, pepper, thyme
1/2 cup butter
12 slices bacon, blanched in boiling water
  and drained
1/2 cup currant jelly, melted

Squeeze lemon juice over birds and into cavities. Rub lightly with oil, sprinkle with salt, pepper, and thyme. Put a knob of butter in each cavity. Press bacon slices lengthwise over breasts of birds and tie them in place with cotton string. Follow directions for smoke cooking poultry on page 173, filling water pan with wine and herbs. When birds are done, snip string, remove bacon, and brush birds with currant jelly. Serve warm, or let cool, wrap in plastic, and refrigerate.
Makes 6 servings

Water pan: 3/4 full
Fire pan: 3/4 full
Smoke-cooking time: 3 to 5 hours
Electric smoker: 3 to 5 hours

By steaming the duck before smoke cooking you get rid of much of the fat—the flesh stays moist and the smoke flavor is delicate. The Chinese sometimes quarter the duck and deep fry it to crisp the skin.

CHINESE TEA DUCK STEAMED AND SMOKED

5- to 6-pound duck
3 tablespoons coarse (kosher) salt
1 teaspoon Szechwan peppercorns
6 slices peeled fresh ginger
4 green onions

Honey-Soy Sauce
1/4 cup hot water
2 tablespoons dark soy sauce
2 tablespoons honey

1/2 cup each raw rice and black tea leaves

Remove fat from cavity of duck and cut off excess skin. Press down on breastbone to flatten duck. Heat salt and peppercorns in a small skillet about 5 minutes, stirring until salt is lightly browned and smoking. Cool. Crush peppercorns. Rub mixture over duck and inside cavity. Put duck in a large bowl and let cure 3 days, turning every day so that it marinates in accumulated salt water. Drain duck and set on a rack in a large kettle or steamer. Top with ginger and onions. Steam over medium heat 1-1/2 hours, replenishing water when necessary. Prick skin of duck in several places with a fork. Pat the duck dry with paper towels. Discard ginger and onions. Degrease juices in steamer and use to fill water pan. Add wood, rice, and tea leaves to the coals. Smoke-cook according to instructions on page 173. Brush duck with Honey-Soy Sauce.
Makes 4 servings

Water pan: 1/2 full
Fire pan: 1/2 full
Smoke-cooking time: 1 hour or more
Electric smoker: 1 hour or more

Even the influence of "Rule Britannia" has not changed the delicacy of smoke cooking in all of Hong Kong and Singapore.

It's better not to stuff the bird for this long slow smoke. Save up your citrus peels to make a pungent smoke to complement the marinade.

SMOKED TURKEY INDIENNE

13- to 18-pound turkey
2-1/2 cups light soy sauce
1 cup sliced green onions
1 cup dry sherry
1/4 cup corn or safflower oil
1 cup chopped fresh parsley
12 cloves garlic, roughly crushed
2 tablespoons curry powder
1 teaspoon cayenne pepper

Remove neck and giblets from cavity of turkey. Rinse turkey and set in a large non-metallic container. Mix remaining ingredients for marinade and pour over turkey. Marinate in the refrigerator up to 36 hours, turning occasionally. Follow directions for smoke cooking poultry, page 173, using marinade with water to fill water pan. Brush with juices in water pan when you replenish smoke and heat, adding water to water pan when necessary. Serve warm, or let cool, wrap in plastic, and refrigerate.
Makes 8 to 10 servings

Water pan: full
Fire pan: heaping
Smoke-cooking time: 10 to 12 hours
Electric smoker: 5 to 6 hours

VERY SIMPLE SMOKE-COOKED TURKEY

8- to 12-pound turkey
A Basic Dry Cure, page 164, or
    A Basic Brine, page 165
1/2 cup butter
1/4 cup corn or safflower oil
2 cloves garlic, crushed
1/4 cup fresh lemon juice
1 teaspoon crumbled dried thyme

Give turkey the basic dry cure or brine treatment. Remove the neck and giblets from the cavity. These can be simmered in the water pan the last 2 hours as the bird finishes cooking. In a small saucepan, melt butter; add oil and garlic. Remove from heat; add lemon juice and thyme. Cool. Dip cheesecloth in butter mixture until saturated. Drape over turkey breast, taking care not to let sides hang down too far. Smoke-cook according to directions on page 173. Baste through cheesecloth with butter mixture whenever you check smoke and water pan. When leg joint moves easily (or a meat thermometer inserted in thigh reads 180°F.), discard cheesecloth, baste again, and serve warm, or let cool and wrap in plastic; refrigerate.
Makes 8 to 10 servings

Water pan: full
Fire pan: heaping
Smoke-cooking time: 10 to 12 hours
Electric smoker: 5 to 6 hours

Flaming apple brandy or melted apple jelly with sage makes a nice finish for a smoke-cooked goose.

CALVADOS-FLAMED SMOKED GOOSE WITH APPLESAUCE

8- to 10-pound goose
A Basic Dry Cure, page 164, or
 A Basic Brine, page 165
Salt and freshly ground pepper
1 large onion
1 large stalk celery with leaves, cut up
1/4 cup Calvados (apple brandy)

Applesauce
4 tart green apples, peeled, cored, and sliced
1/2 cup water
1/2 cup Calvados
1/4 cup butter
1/4 cup sugar
Salt and grated nutmeg

Treat the goose with basic dry cure or brine. Pat dry. Remove all visible fat and reserve for basting. Season the cavity and place onion and celery inside. Puncture the skin in several places, especially below the legs and breast, to allow fat to run off. Pat some of the reserved fat over breasts. Follow smoke cooking instructions on page 173. Smoke-cook until leg moves easily in joint. Remove from smoker. Discard onion and celery. Warm brandy, ignite carefully, and pour over goose. To make applesauce: In a saucepan, cook apples in water and brandy, covered, until tender. Mash coarsely. Add butter, sugar, a pinch of salt and nutmeg. Serve warm or cold with goose.

Water pan: full
Fire pan: full
Smoke-cooking time: 7 to 8 hours
Electric smoker: 30 to 45 minutes per pound

SMOKE-COOKING CHART FOR MEAT
Smoker Temperature for Meat: 200°-225°F.

TYPE OF MEAT	WEIGHT IN LB.	HOURS TO SMOKE: CHARCOAL	HOURS TO SMOKE: ELECTRIC	TEMPERATURE WHEN COOKED
Roasts: beef	3-4	4-5	25-30 min. per lb.	140°F. rare
Roasts: beef	5-7	5-6	25-30 min. per lb.	160°F. med.
Roasts: beef	8-10	7-8	25-30 min. per lb.	170°F. well
Roasts: pork	3-4	5-6	45-60 min. per lb.	170°F. well
Roasts: pork	5-8	7-8	45-60 min. per lb.	170°F. well
Butterflied leg of lamb	5-7	5-9	25-30 min. per lb.	145°F.
Lamb shoulder	5-7	5-6	25-30 min. per lb.	145°F.
Chops: lamb		3-4	45 min. per lb.	145°F.
Chops: pork		4-6	45 min. per lb.	170°F.
Ribs: pork	5	4-6	3-4 hr. total time	
Ham: cooked	all	3-4	45-60 min. per lb.	130°F.
Ham: fresh	10	7-8	45-60 min. per lb.	170°F.
Sweetbreads		2-3	1-1/2 - 2 hr.	
Calves liver		3-5	1-1/2 - 2 hr.	
Meatloaf, pâté	2-4	2-4	2-4 hr.	160°F.

SMOKE COOKING MEAT

1. If you like, give meat the basic dry cure or brine treatment (see page 165 for times), or marinate for 3 hours at room temperature or up to 30 hours in the refrigerator.

2. Pour charcoal briquettes into fire pan and ignite (prepare a separate pan of coals to reserve for a long smoke).

3. Soak 1 to 4 chunks of wood or 1/2 to 1 quart of wood chips in water for about 20 minutes.

4. When coals are completely covered with gray ash (about 30 minutes), drain the wood on paper towels and add some to coals (reserve some wood for later use). (Electric units may have a special pan for dry wood.)

5. Set water pan in place. Fill with any reserved marinade and enough hot water to almost fill pan.

6. Spray grill with non-stick coating or rub with vegetable oil and set in place.

7. Center meat on grill over water pan. Brush with marinade or vegetable oil (plug in electric smoker.)

8. Make sure temperature is steady between 200° and 225°F. Add hot coals to increase temperature or remove a few coals to decrease temperature. Add soaked wood to maintain a steady stream of smoke.

9. Each time you check the smoke, blot surface of meat with a paper towel and brush with marinade or vegetable oil.

10. Continue smoking until desired doneness. Serve warm or let cool to room temperature. To store, cool, wrap airtight, and refrigerate.

You can add vegetables to the water pan to cook during the last hour or so of smoke cooking.

SMOKE-ROASTED BEEF
In a Good Burgundian Marinade

3- to 4-pound beef roast

Burgundian Marinade
3 cups dry red wine
Grated zest and juice of 2 lemons
2 bay leaves
2 whole cloves
6 black peppercorns, crushed
1 large onion, sliced
3 carrots, chopped
3 ribs celery with leaves, chopped
3 cloves garlic, crushed
Pinch of thyme, tarragon, salt, and sugar

Place roast in a glass or other non-metallic bowl or a heavy plastic bag. Combine remaining ingredients and pour over beef; cover and refrigerate overnight, turning several times in marinade. Remove meat and drain on paper towels. Smoke-cook according to instructions on page 180; use marinade with water in water pan. When beef is cooked, use marinade as a sauce.
Makes 8 servings

Water pan: 3/4 full
Fire pan: 3/4 full
Smoke-cooking time: 4 to 5 hours
Electric smoker: 25 to 35 minutes per pound

Wonderful for a new version of Reuben sandwich, this brisket is braised before smoking.

CORNED BEEF BRISKET
With a Smoky Edge

3- to 4-pound corned beef brisket
1/2 cup each sliced carrots and celery with leaves
1 large onion, quartered
1 teaspoon each salt and pepper
2 whole cloves

Mustard Glaze
3 tablespoons Dijon-style mustard
2 tablespoons brown sugar
2 tablespoons sour cream
2 tablespoons ground cinnamon

Place beef in kettle with vegetables and seasonings. Add water to cover. Bring to a boil, cover, and simmer 2 hours. Drain. Pat dry with paper towels. Follow directions for smoke cooking on page 180, allowing 2 hours or more for cooking, until brisket is tender. When the brisket has 15 minutes to go mix together ingredients for mustard glaze and brush it over brisket.
Makes 8 servings

Water pan: 3/4 full
Fire pan: 3/4 full
Smoke-cooking time: 2 to 4 hours
Electric smoker: 25 to 30 minutes per pound

SMOKE-COOKED LOIN OF PORK
WITH A FRESH ROSEMARY SMOKE

5- to 7-pound boned pork loin, rolled and tied
A Basic Dry Cure, page 164, or
 A Basic Brine, page 165
1/2 cup olive oil
2 cloves garlic, crushed
1/2 teaspoon crushed hot red pepper
1 teaspoon crumbled dried thyme
Brush of fresh rosemary
 (or 2 teaspoons dried rosemary)

Give pork the basic cure or brine treatment. Follow directions for smoke cooking on page 180. Toss a few branches of rosemary on the coals. Mix oil, garlic, red pepper, and thyme in a small bowl. Steep rosemary brush in oil mixture. Brush roast several times before smoke cooking, during cooking when you check smoke and fire, and after the roast is done. Serve warm or let cool, wrap in plastic, and refrigerate.
Makes 12 servings

Water pan: full
Fire pan: full
Smoke-cooking time: 7 to 8 hours
Electric smoker: 45 to 60 minutes per pound

It may seem difficult to imagine the steamer Atlanta *once plying the placid waters of Lake Titticaca, but the Uro Indian maiden still smokes strips of* charqui *over a greenwood fire, as did her Incan ancestors.*

SMOKED PORK OR BEEF RIBS
WITH THE DEVIL'S OWN SAUCE

5 to 6 pounds meaty pork or beef ribs
1/3 cup sea or coarse (kosher) salt
1/3 cup brown sugar, lightly packed
2 tablespoons coarsely ground black pepper
1 tablespoon grated lemon zest
2 teaspoons Tabasco sauce
1 tablespoon paprika

Devil's Own Sauce
1 cup beef broth
1/2 cup Worcestershire sauce
1/3 cup cider vinegar
1/3 cup corn or safflower oil
1 teaspoon each dry mustard, chili powder,
 and paprika
 2 to 3 teaspoons Tabasco sauce

Rub ribs with mixture of salt, brown sugar, pepper, lemon peel, Tabasco sauce, and paprika. Cover and refrigerate overnight. Follow directions for smoke cooking on page 180. Bring all ingredients for sauce to a boil in a small saucepan. Brush ribs with sauce, basting each time you check smoke and after you remove ribs from smoker.
Makes 6 servings

Water pan: full
Fire pan: full
Smoke-cooking time: 4 to 6 hours
Electric smoker: 45 minutes per pound

BABY BACK RIBS MARINATED IN BEER

1 quart beer
2 cups dark brown sugar, lightly packed
1 cup cider vinegar
1 tablespoon each chili powder, ground cumin, and dry mustard
2 teaspoons salt
2 teaspoons crushed hot red pepper
2 bay leaves
6 slabs trimmed pork baby back ribs (about 2 pounds each)
Ketchup

Combine beer, sugar, vinegar, chili powder, cumin, dry mustard, salt, red pepper, and bay leaves in a large pan; bring to a boil, remove from heat, and cool. Place ribs in a large shallow roasting pan; pour marinade over ribs, turning several times while they marinate about 24 hours in refrigerator. Drain ribs, reserving marinade. Arrange ribs on grill or rib rack and smoke-cook according to directions on page 180 until meat is tender, basting with marinade whenever you check smoke. When meat is tender, brush with a little ketchup to glaze.
Makes 6 servings

Water pan: full
Fire pan: full
Smoke-cooking time: 7 to 8 hours
Electric smoker: 45 to 60 minutes per pound

BLACK RASPBERRY SOY MARINADE FOR PORK AND DUCK

1-1/2 cups black raspberry liqueur
2/3 cup white wine vinegar
1/3 cup corn or safflower oil
2 tablespoons soy sauce

Mix ingredients in a bowl and keep in the refrigerator to marinate and baste pork and duck.
Makes 1 pint

A MINT AND GARLIC MARINADE FOR LAMB CHOPS

4 cloves garlic, crushed
1/3 cup each red wine vinegar and vegetable oil
1 tablespoon each sherry wine and soy sauce
1/4 cup fresh or dried mint leaves, chopped
1 bay leaf, crumbled

Combine all ingredients in a glass bowl. Add lamb chops, cover and marinate several hours, turning several times in marinade. Drain lamb on paper towels. Use marinade with water in water pan when smoke cooking lamb.

Garlic, onions, and eggplant are three of the few vegetables that can take a smoke satisfactorily. Coincidentally they are all wonderful with lamb.

SMOKE-COOKED BUTTERFLIED LEG OF LAMB
With Smoky Heads of Garlic

5- to 6-pound leg of lamb, boned and butterflied
1/2 cup corn or safflower oil
1 cup teriyaki sauce
1/2 cup fresh lemon juice
2 teaspoons sugar
3 cloves garlic, crushed
2 tablespoons chopped mixed fresh herbs
6 Smoky Heads of Garlic, following

Marinate lamb overnight in mixture of oil, teriyaki sauce, lemon juice, sugar, crushed garlic, and herbs. Prepare heads of garlic. Follow directions for smoke cooking on page 180 (lamb is best smoke-cooked to medium-rare), brushing with marinade before and after cooking. Serve warm, sliced thinly on the diagonal. Pass heads of garlic to squeeze over lamb and warm French bread.
Makes 6 servings

Water pan: full
Fire pan: 3/4 full
Smoke-cooking time: 5 to 6 hours
Electric smoker: 15 to 20 minutes per pound

Whole heads of garlic can be smoke-cooked along with other foods. Great for squeezing over warm buttered French bread or for seasoning vegetables and meats.

SMOKY HEADS OF GARLIC

4 whole heads of garlic
8 tablespoons soft butter
1/4 cup chopped fresh parsley

Peel back most of the papery skins from the outer cloves of garlic. Rub butter over all. Set on grill with other foods and smoke-cook 2 hours or more. Sprinkle with parsley before serving.

SMOKE-COOKED ONIONS

6 medium onions
1/4 cup corn or safflower oil
Chopped fresh or crumbled dried herbs
Butter

Remove outer skins of onions. Rub with oil and herbs. Set on grill the last 2 or 3 hours of smoke cooking any of your other foods. When tender, quarter onions, taking care not to slice completely through. Insert a knob of butter in center of each and sprinkle with more herbs.
Makes 6 servings

A SMOKY CAPONATA

2 smoke-cooked onions, page 185
1 head smoke-cooked garlic, page 185
1 eggplant (about 1-1/2 pounds), cut into
  thick slices with peel
1/3 cup olive oil
1 cup sliced celery
2 tablespoons tomato paste
1 can (15 ounces) whole peeled tomatoes,
  with liquid
1/2 cup each black and green olives, pitted
1/2 cup toasted pine nuts
1 teaspoon each fennel seed, dill weed,
  salt, pepper, and red wine vinegar

See recipes for smoke cooking onions and garlic. When onions and garlic are almost tender, arrange eggplant slices on grill and continue smoking 20 to 30 minutes. Remove outer peel of onions and slice into wedges. Cut eggplant into chunks. Squeeze garlic cloves into a saucepan with oil and celery. Sauté 2 minutes. Add remaining ingredients and simmer until mixture has thickened, about 20 minutes. Stir in onion and eggplant. Let cool and refrigerate overnight. Correct seasonings.
Makes 8 servings

Large cuts of game with little fat need to be larded with salt pork or bacon before smoking.

SMOKED HAUNCH OF VENISON

8- to 10-pound haunch of venison
1/2 pound salt pork, cut into 1/4-inch strips
6 cloves garlic, halved
Two recipes Burgundian Marinade, page 181
1 cup red or black currant jelly
Salt and coarsely ground pepper

Use a larding needle to thoroughly lard the haunch with strips of salt pork. Insert garlic halves in shallow slashes. Make up double the amount of Burgundian Marinade and pour over venison in a large earthenware crock or non-metallic bowl. Marinate overnight. Smoke-cook venison fat side up, using marinade in water pan, following instructions for smoke cooking on page 180. When venison is cooked to desired doneness, remove water pan and prepare a sauce with the drippings and currant jelly, thickening the mixture, if you wish, and seasoning it to taste.

Water pan: full
Fire pan: full
Smoke-cooking time: 7 to 8 hours
Electric smoker: 25 to 30 minutes per pound

"For this I will set down. A glowing hickory-wood chip fire and a pan of bouillon, all in a heavy black iron cauldron, will produce an succulent shank of smoked venison. . . ."

SMOKED COUNTRY PÂTÉ

1 pound beef or pork liver
2 pounds lean pork shoulder
1 pound unsalted fatback
2 onions
6 cloves garlic
1 cup parsley sprigs
4 slices white bread, trimmed
1/2 cup milk
6 eggs, lightly beaten
1 tablespoon salt
2 teaspoon Quatre Épices, following
1 teaspoon coarse black pepper
6 slices bacon

Cut meat, fatback, and onions into small chunks for meat grinder or food processor. Grind meat with onions, garlic, and parsley through coarsest blade. In a large bowl, soak bread in milk, stir in eggs, spices, and ground meat. Spoon into an oiled glazed earthenware baking dish or 10-inch-deep pie pan, depending on the space you have in the smoker. Top loaf with slices of bacon. Smoke-cook until a skewer inserted in middle of loaf comes out clean. Pour off excess liquid. Serve warm, or let cool, wrap in plastic, and refrigerate. To serve, slice thin and serve with mustard and pickles.
Makes 10 to 12 servings

Water pan: 3/4 full
Fire pan: 3/4 full
Smoke-cooking time: 4 to 5 hours
Electric smoker: 4 hours

QUATRE ÉPICES

1 tablespoon ground cinnamon
1 tablespoon ground allspice
1 teaspoon ground cloves
2 teaspoons grated nutmeg
4 teaspoons ground coriander

Blend all ingredients and store in a jar with a tight-fitting lid.

SMOKED WHOLE CALVES LIVER WITH GARLIC

1 whole calves liver
3 cloves garlic, slivered
Burgundian Marinade, page 181
3 to 4 strips bacon
Chopped tarragon or other herbs
Lemon wedges

Rinse liver and pat dry with paper towels. Make small incisions with tip of knife and insert slivers of garlic. Cover with Burgundian Marinade and let stand 2 hours or more. Follow directions for smoke cooking on page 180. Set liver on grill and arrange bacon over surface. Smoke until done to your taste, preferably on the rosy side. Remove bacon and crumble over top with herbs. Slice very thin and serve with lemon wedges.
Makes 12 servings

Water pan: 2/3 full
Fire pan: 1/2 full
Smoke-cooking time: 2 to 4 hours
Electric smoker: 25 to 30 minutes per pound

INDEX

BIOGRAPHICAL NOTES

MAGGIE WALDRON's life has been devoted to culinary interests. She grew up in the restaurant-hotel business and graduated from Cornell and La Varenne cooking school in Paris. She has been an associate food editor at McCall's, a television director for a major food company, and the principal in her own consulting firm. As Vice President-Food Director, Creative Services for Ketchum Communications, she is the creative spark of Maggie's Kitchen, where recipes are developed and photographed for some of the nation's leading producers of food and wine. Her work appears regularly in magazines, newspapers, and on film. Throughout her career she has worked with, studied with, or become friends with many of the world's best-known and most talented cooks, who have shared their recipes with her for this book.

ERNI YOUNG, during an outstandingly prolific thirty-year career, has worked simultaneously as an artist, interior architect, planner, and graphic designer. Presently he is the principal of Erni Young NSCA/IBD Associates, Designers, Consultants and Planners. He is also an Associate Professor in the Interior Architectural Design Department at the California College of Arts and Crafts, Oakland/San Francisco. His fine art commissions include drawings, paintings, murals, and sculpture for numerous hospitals and other public buildings throughout California and the West Coast, in a wide variety of media from bas relief and leaded glass to painted tapestries.